PELICAN BOOKS

A878

FREUD AND CHRISTIANITY

Roy Stuart Lee spent his boyhood years in the Australian bush. He was educated at Orange High School and Sydney University, and later at Oxford University, receiving the degrees of M.A., B.Litt. and D.Phil. He was Vice-Warden of St John's College, Morpeth, New South Wales, but he came back to England in 1938 and worked at St Martin-in-the-Fields, London. During the war he was chaplain to No. 1 Central London Clearing Station, and he served through all the bombing raids of the Blitz. After some time as Overseas religious broadcasting organizer for the B.B.C. he was appointed vicar of the University Church of St Mary the Virgin, Oxford. He is now Fellow and Chaplain of St Catherine's College, Oxford, and he is also Chaplain of Nuffield College.

While still at Sydney University he held a science Research Scholarship in Psychology concurrently with his theological studies. This stimulated his interest in the relationship of psychology and religion, which has remained a major study throughout his life. He has lectured extensively on it in Britain, Australia and the United States. He has also published *Psychology and Worship* and *Your Growing Child and Religion* (available as a Pelican). He is married and has two daughters.

R. S. LEE

FREUD AND CHRISTIANITY

PENGUIN BOOKS

Penguin Books Ltd, Harmondsworth, Middlesex, England
Penguin Books Australia Ltd, Ringwood, Victoria, Australia

—

First published by James Clarke & Co. Ltd 1948
Published in Pelican Books 1967

—

Copyright © R. S. Lee, 1948

—

Made and printed in Great Britain
by Hunt Barnard & Co. Ltd, Aylesbury
Set in Monotype Imprint

CONTENTS

EDITORIAL FOREWORD

FOR many people psychoanalysis and Christianity are incompatible. In fact some commentators have claimed that the spread of Freud's ideas has been responsible for a decline in religious belief and practice. Freud was a determinist. He believed that all aspects of behaviour and experience had their causes, that free will was an illusion, and that life could be understood without recourse to explanations in terms of a spiritual world. He believed further that a child's early experience of his parents helped to determine his idea of God, and that other religious beliefs were prompted by anxiety and wishful thinking.

Despite all this, there are many psychologists and psychiatrists who believe in God, and there are many religious believers who see the merits of psychoanalysis. Some people keep these beliefs parallel and separate: they try to get the best of both worlds by keeping them in separate compartments. Dr Lee, who is a minister of religion and who has a profound knowledge of psychoanalysis, has been particularly successful in taking the more difficult path of integrating the two systems of belief. He takes the view that there are some aspects of religion which can be explained in the way Freud proposed, and that the practising Christian is all the better for having insight into his own and his church's underlying motives. As a result his religion will be purer and closer to Christ's teaching.

The reader of this book is not expected to have any prior knowledge of psychoanalysis, but if he has, the author's clear exposition will refresh his view; and he will certainly gain in his understanding of Christianity.

B. M. FOSS

PREFACE

In writing this book I have attempted to open up a field of thought which has been too much neglected. I believe in what I understand to be Christianity, that through Christ and his teachings man can find the highest fulfilment of life. I believe also that psychoanalysis as developed by Freud gives us a more accurate insight into the working of the mind than does any other psychology. Because I believe in the worth of both, I believe they are reconcilable. I have therefore set out to show a few, but only a few, of the connexions which seem to me to exist between them. I have confined myself to this. I have not attempted to prove the claim of Christianity to set forth truth. I have not attempted to demonstrate the soundness of psychoanalysis, nor to give a systematic exposition of it. I have no doubt that many Christians will think that I have given an inadequate presentation of Christianity and as many psychoanalysts accuse me of distorting or abusing the teaching of Freud in making it appear to support Christianity. Those who want proof of psychoanalysis and Christianity must seek it elsewhere. If they read further in this book, all I hope they will find will be the demonstration of how psychoanalysis can cleanse Christianity of non-Christian elements and can give it deeper insights into the true qualities of human life. Assuming both to be true, I have tried to draw some of the inferences necessary. I put them forward tentatively in the hope that they may stimulate others to develop the subject more thoroughly.

I am very conscious of the inadequacies and omissions which the reader will find. I have been forced to these by my own shortcomings and by the limits to which the study has had to be confined. I have thought it advisable to give a condensed account of the simplest discoveries of psychoanalysis for the sake of readers who have little acquaintance with it. This has meant drastic simplification, so drastic as at times to be misleading. The human mind is infinitely complex and to attempt to follow all the variants of any particular type of mental process would have prevented us from getting anywhere at all. The selection of material has therefore had to be governed by this principle of simplicity for the sake of clarity. Thus I have left out of consideration the development of the feminine outlook, different in profound ways from the masculine to which I have confined the study. Yet the study of Christianity without the study of its appeal to women is a very mutilated treatment of the subject. In spite of these grave defects, the book will have served its purpose if it convinces some students that there is a real connexion between the work of Freud and of the great Christian teachers and persuades them to think a little further about it.

The plan of treatment has involved occasional repetition where I felt that it was useful to emphasize the point and simpler than to refer the reader to the relevant passages. I can only hope the reader will not find the repetition tiresome.

Two of my friends, Professor L. W. Grensted, of Oxford, and the Right Reverend E. H. Burgmann, Bishop of Goulburn, will recognize how much they have influenced my thinking, but I would not like them to be held responsible for the views put forward. Finally, I have to express my deep gratitude to my friend and secretary, Mrs J. Upton-Hunn, for her invaluable assistance to me in preparing the book for the press.

R. S. L.

St Martin-in-the-Fields,
  London.

CHAPTER I

INTRODUCTION

THIS book aims to discuss some of the more obvious ways in which the knowledge of the human mind that we have gained through psychoanalysis throws light upon traditional Christian religion, its beliefs, its aspirations, its emotions, sentiments and practices. We can say at once that it contributes much to the understanding of religion, both in a general form – that is, the place of religion in human life – and also on particular issues, such as, to quote an example at random, the doctrine of original sin. Indeed, we may even see it as a very strong challenge to orthodox religion. Freud's essay, *The Future of an Illusion*, embodies a very powerful general criticism of the validity of religious beliefs which cannot be ignored. At least we can be sure that the result of applying psychoanalysis to their understanding is likely to be some profound modifications in religious thought and practice.

The bearing of psychoanalysis upon the validity of religious experience is a special aspect of the wider problem of science and religion about which there has been so much argument in the last hundred years and on which it is certain the last word has not yet been said. The problem used mostly to be stated as 'the conflict between science and religion', and argued as if both could not be true at the same time. If science was right, religion must be wrong, and vice versa. It is in this form that we still frequently meet it. Nevertheless, right from the beginning there have been scientists and theologians who saw no conflict. However, since psychoanalysis is often presented as refuting religious belief, it is advisable for us, before we come to the special problem of psychoanalysis, to glance briefly at the salient points of the century-old argument.

The so-called conflict is usually described as beginning with Galileo, who challenged the belief that the earth is the centre of the universe when he claimed, following Copernicus, that the earth moves round the sun. Theologians had used the prevailing belief, which seemed self-evident to the senses, that the sun moves round the earth, as establishing the importance of the earth, and so of man, in the scheme of God's creation. Galileo's teaching therefore was assailed as a criticism of the teaching of the Bible that man is the highest of God's creations. The conflict developed a stage further when geologists, studying the stratification and origin of rocks, particularly fossil remains, set up a time chart for the age of the earth which called for millions of years instead of the 4004 B.C. which the accepted chronology of the Old Testament gave as the date of the Creation. The battle rose to its climax when Darwin advanced his theory of the evolution of plants and animals and so challenged the truth of the creation stories of the Book of Genesis. As a result of the controversies which have raged since then the true nature of the problem has gradually been defined and a number of points have emerged which it is important to bear in mind in relation to the fresh controversies springing up around the new sciences, such as psychoanalysis.

In the first place, the scientists have almost invariably been right on matters of fact and the defenders of religion, or rather, of the literal truth of the Book of Genesis, wrong. The work of the physicists and astronomers, the geological account of the earth's formation and the theory of evolution are now accepted almost universally, subject to such corrections as the sciences themselves make. It is recognized now that it is the province of science to determine facts and their connexions. If the theory of evolution should have to be given up, it can only be on scientific grounds. Religion may ask science to check its findings, but it has got out of its proper sphere if in opposition to science it claims the right to make independent assertions about matters of fact. This does not mean, of course, that religion is not interested in factual accuracy. On the contrary, that is very important to religion. All it means is that religion, as religion, is bound to accept the facts which science declares to be accurate.

Secondly, religion must be distinguished from the false theories about facts which have been associated with it or which it has assumed without question from current thought, even though some theologians may refuse to draw the distinction and uphold those theories in the name of religion. In the controversies in question partisans on each side argued as if Christianity was proved completely false when the creation stories were shown to be inaccurate as factual history. There is truth in these stories, but it is religious truth. That is, they are parables or myths expressing the relation of God to the world. Religious truth is concerned with ultimate meanings, expressed in terms of values, judgements of worth. It is not concerned primarily with scientific truth. Of course, truthfulness about fact is one of the values which religion upholds and religious truth must have its basis in scientific truth. It transcends but must include scientific truth in its order of values.

The third point which has clearly and indisputably emerged is that dogmatism has not been all on the side of religion. There have been many scientists who have claimed too much in their zeal to defend the right of science to plough up holy ground. They have asserted that the scientific approach to facts is the only one; that the religious approach, emphasizing faith in a spiritual order of values, is superstition and its values simply irrational emotionalism. They have thus in their turn carried science out of its proper province of determining and explaining facts and they have as individuals made value judgements on the basis of their scientific knowledge, judgements which they have mistaken for science. The criticism which they passed on religion was not scientific at all. Science, up to the present revolutionary phase of physics, has implicitly assumed mechanistic materialism as the structure of the universe and imported that background into the argument with religion, mistakenly believing it to be science. Hence the controversies usually became a dispute between two philosophies, not between science and religion. In such a dispute religion was on surer ground. That mechanistic materialism is not a necessary part of science is shown by the progress of the modern physical sciences which have thrown it over in favour of relativity, four-dimensional space-time, the quantum theory and the statistical concept in place of absolute determinism or the finality of cause and effect. Scientists of today – at any rate, physicists and astronomers – seem far less inclined to be dogmatic than their predecessors of last century. They are not thereby less 'scientific'.

Lastly, the problem of the relation of science and religion can be stated in its essential terms once it is recognized that religion is not concerned to refute science and science is not a substitute for religion. They are two different activities of the human spirit, not as rivals competing for the total allegiance of the mind, but complementary to each other and indeed essential to each other for the full development of man. Science establishes what is fact and demonstrates the connexions between facts. Religion constructs an order of values to be expressed in and to direct every activity of man – thoughts, feelings, or actions. It derives this order of values from an interpretation of the whole universe and of man's place in it. If the interpretation of the universe is built on false foundations through rejection of knowledge or deliberate acceptance of inaccuracy, the system of values derived from it is sure to prove unsatisfactory in various ways. Hence religion depends upon science to supply it with the most accurate and extensive information possible. Religion shapes the ends men seek to fulfil in the world, science supplies knowledge about the world.

This states the problem in its simplest form. In practice religion cannot wait till science has completed its work, nor can an individual wait to acquire an extensive knowledge based on science before he forms religious beliefs and shapes his life towards religious ends. Religion and science must grow up together, both historically and in the individual, and they must constantly interact and modify each other.

We must note a further important complication. Religious beliefs and practices are facts even though they embody values, and as such they come into the normal province of science to be studied in a scientific way. For religion they are very important facts, so the scientific study of religion is essential to the well-being of religion.

It is in this respect that psychoanalysis is specially relevant.

Not only does it provide essential general information about the nature of man, with whom religion is supremely concerned, it also subjects man's religious behaviour to a minute analysis as part of his general activity. As a result of this study psychoanalysis is able to provide some criteria by which to assess the worth of particular religious manifestations. Its chief contribution to religion, however, will be in the light it can shed on the development and functioning of the human mind and character, thus providing religion with sound knowledge on which to shape its ideals, its judgements, and its interpretation of man's place in the universe.

Psychoanalysis can do this in so far as it is a science and so can lay claim to speak with authority about the facts of human behaviour. But if it is a science, and we may concede this at once, it must be subject to the limitations of science and relinquish any claim to be a judge in the sphere of ultimate values. In the essay referred to above, *The Future of an Illusion*, Freud was scrupulously careful to define the sense in which he used the term 'illusion', a special psychological sense (pp. 53–5), and he added (p. 57): 'It does not lie within the scope of this enquiry to estimate the value of religious doctrines as truth.' That is true of psychoanalysis as a whole. It may challenge the truth or adequacy of assertions about fact made in the guise of religion, or of assumptions on which religious doctrines are based, or it may question the factual interpretation of a particular religious experience, such as a vision, but as psychoanalysis it cannot pronounce on the ultimate truth and validity of religion. It must fall into line with the other sciences out of which the conflict with religion first sprang.

This point has been raised here to help define the limits within which we can expect to get fruitful results from an enquiry into the relations of psychoanalysis and religion. We need to have the perspective clear from the beginning. Confusion already exists about it. In spite of his disclaimer cited above, Freud seems to assert, and many of his followers definitely assert, that his arguments disprove religion. It would be a pity if all the old arguments have to be worked through once more and the bearing of psychoanalysis on religion confused in the same way as happened over evolution, just because psychoanalysts claim too much for their science and theologians cling to error, believing it to be essential to their faith. The writer does not intend to fight over old ground battles already decided. In the following chapters it will be assumed that psychoanalysis takes its status as a science and as such searches out truths of fact about the human mind. Religion as religion must accept the facts which psycho-analysis establishes scientifically and upon them, with truths derived from other sciences, build its system of values which it endeavours to exemplify in conduct. Its interpretation of the universe must not deny the truths which psychoanalysis demonstrates.

In the next four chapters some of the main findings of psychoanalysis will be explained without any attempt to prove them. These chapters cannot of course be considered as an introduction to psychoanalysis or even a summary of its dis-coveries. They select for emphasis some of the more im-portant features which can be explained fairly simply. The second half of the book, from Chapter 6 onwards, goes back over the ground covered in the first half to examine the relevance of the main points on Christian belief and practice. We may expect to find that false theories about the nature of the human mind have crept into religion and been accepted without question. If this is so it will only be a repetition of what happened when the earlier sciences of astronomy, geology and biology sprang up. The Christian religion has gained in richness from the scientific knowledge those sciences brought. So will it prove in the case of psychoanalysis also. Clearing away the weeds allows the garden to bear richer fruit.

Part One

PSYCHOANALYSIS

CHAPTER 2

WHAT IS PSYCHOANALYSIS?

PSYCHOANALYSIS will always be associated with the name of Sigmund Freud. He was the pioneer in opening up this field of study and his contribution to it far outstrips that of any other worker in the field. His discovery and elaboration of psychoanalysis entitle him to rank with Darwin and Einstein as exceptional leaders in different branches of science. Darwin by his *Origin of Species* cleared the way for the scientific study of the evolution of plants and animals. Einstein's formulation of the theory of relativity began a new epoch in physics. Their work became the fundamental basis from which all further study in biology and physics developed. They are great landmarks in the history of their sciences. It is the same with Freud. Psychoanalysis has brought about a radical change in the study of human behaviour and in the conceptions of psychology. It has thrown new light on old problems and opened up new fields for investigation. Not the least important aspect of psychoanalysis is the way in which it flows over into every sphere of human behaviour and finds rich material for study, as well as scope for practical application, in literature, art, medicine, anthropology, economics, politics, religion and all the social sciences. In this short book we shall have to confine ourselves to tracing out some of the ways in which it bears on Christianity, to discover how far accepted Christian doctrines and practices require modification as a result of the understanding which psychoanalysis has brought of the working of the human mind.

Freud's first major formulation of his theories is to be found in *The Interpretation of Dreams*, published at the beginning of this century. Since then he and his followers have developed and extended his early work and have modified some of his earlier conclusions, sometimes quite considerably. The most important of Freud's later publications is *The Ego and the Id*, but to get a thorough grasp of Freudian psychoanalysis it is necessary to follow the development of his thought by reading at least his main works in order of their appearance. Each succeeding volume presupposes a knowledge of the argument of the earlier ones and proceeds to develop or correct that argument without always stating it for the sake of new readers. The student is therefore faced with the situation that he cannot always follow the latest volumes without reading the earlier, and if he reads only the earlier he may find himself accepting, or rejecting, theories already thrown overboard by Freud himself in his later works.

Freud did his early work on psychoanalysis almost entirely alone. Soon, however, he attracted followers to himself, among them Jung and Adler, now famous names in psychology. After working with Freud for some years each of these in turn left him to pursue independent lines of investigation. They rejected some of the conclusions which Freud regarded as essential to sound psychoanalytic practice and theory and in their turn they advanced theories which Freud (and others) pronounce fallacious or misleading because presenting at best only part of the truth. Since then other investigators, usually drawing their inspiration in the first place from Freud, have also become 'heretics' in psychoanalysis or have developed systems and doctrines of their own based to a greater or lesser degree upon Freudian principles. In England, William Brown and J. A. Hadfield are the best known of this group, if group it may be called. Others again try to adopt an eclectic approach, taking from this or that system of psychology whatever appeals to them, trying to combine the diverse elements into a single scheme, usually with only a superficial success, which may, however, be misleading to beginners in what is frequently called 'Modern Psychology'.

At one time psychoanalysis almost became a popular craze. Certainly a great many people tried to get some knowledge about it and some experience of its working, and terms and ideas supposed to be derived from it frequently found a place in popular literature of all kinds. As a result terms like 'the unconscious', 'repression', 'complex', 'sublimation', have become part of everyday language. It must be said at once that the popular use of such terms, like the popular idea of psycho-analysis, is usually an inaccurate representation of their scientific meaning. It is on a par with the widespread presumption that because Jung and Adler and Freud use rather similar terminology the differences between their teachings do not amount to much. Such loose use of terms and such ill-founded generalizations constitute a severe handicap to students approaching the subject.

It is because far too much has been written or spoken that passes for psychoanalysis and is not psychoanalysis at all that we must first attempt a brief answer to the question, 'What is psychoanalysis?'

Psychoanalysis began as a method of treating certain kinds of mental disorder and is still chiefly a psychotherapeutic technique, that is, a method of healing by psychological means. It was discovered by Freud in his search to understand and treat hysteria. His attention had been attracted to a special case in which a colleague had departed, almost unintentionally, from the current form of treatment and in which to his surprise he had effected a cure. This colleague did not understand the significance of his success and there were circumstances about the case, easily explicable in terms of developed psychoanalytic theory, which made him unwilling to examine the case further or pursue the method with other cases. When Freud gave it close investigation he soon realized that the success was due to certain features of the new method into which his colleague had drifted by chance. He experimented with it and developed it into a highly successful technique.

At this stage he was only feeling his way more or less blindly and he later admitted that he was lucky to have had so large a measure of success before he understood more fully what was happening in the minds of his patients and the reasons why the method should be successful. There was nothing in the current psychology to explain it. Freud had to develop theory and practice together. The new technique required for its theoretical justification the introduction of some new ideas about the structure and functioning of the mind. It seemed to presuppose that underneath the conscious mind there is a very active unconscious mind with which the conscious mind is in conflict, but in such a way that the conscious mind is unaware not only of the unconscious but also of the conflict. Freud therefore formulated his two basic ideas of 'the unconscious' and 'repression', ideas which were revolutionary at the time, but which are now almost universally accepted by psychologists.

The new conceptions not only explained the success of the new technique, they also helped to improve it and to indicate ways in which it could be used with more precision at each stage of the treatment. Improvement in technique brought further facts to light which enabled Freud to clarify, modify and develop his theories. This again reacted on the technique, which was further refined and extended. Each gain in technique or theory led to an advance in the other.

We can understand this readily enough if we glance briefly at some of the basic ideas of psychoanalysis. They will be dealt with more fully at a later stage. Here it is enough to see their general significance. Our minds as we know them by direct introspection consist of what is in consciousness at the moment and the store of memories and other mental processes which flow readily into consciousness at the appropriate stimulus or association. But this is not the whole of the mind. Behind this conscious system, or beneath it (spatial metaphors are misleading about the mind), there is the unconscious mind of which we have no direct knowledge. It is a vast storehouse of unremembered past experiences with an active, fermenting life of its own and its own characteristic ways of functioning. The unconscious mind, or the unconscious as it is usually termed, is continually striving to break into consciousness and take control of the bodily organs of expression and action. The unconscious impulses are prevented from becoming conscious and passing into action by the process of repression. Repression is the activity of the mind which keeps the unconscious unconscious by preventing anything passing from it into the conscious mind except under special conditions it imposes. A rough analogy likens repression to a censorship guarding the frontiers of consciousness, deleting or altering what it does not approve.

Repression is a dynamic force and not merely a sieve to sift what has to pass through it. It is more like a counter-attack than a barricade. If the impulses coming from the unconscious are powerful and persistent, the strength of the repressing forces has also to be powerful and persistent to resist and overcome them. As both groups of forces draw from the common supply of the energy of the mind, any individual whose repressions are severe finds himself exhausted by the conflict. But he does not know why, for the conflict is unconscious. If he knew what it was he was repressing, the unconscious forces would have already gained their end before the battle began and become conscious. Repression would have failed. Instead, both the rejected impulses and the process of repressing them are kept outside consciousness. Repression, therefore, does not mean controlling impulses which we consciously judge to be undesirable. It is most important to grasp this clearly. If psychoanalysis is to be understood and its implications realized, we must avoid the common misinterpretation of the technical term 'repression'. Conscious rejection of undesired impulses may be called 'suppression' or 'control', perhaps 'self-control'. Repression is the unconscious process which keeps the unconscious mind what it is, not conscious.

Certain disorders of the mind have their source in this conflict of consciousness and the unconscious. These are called 'neuroses' or 'psychoneuroses'. They differ from mental diseases caused by injury or deficiency of the nervous tissue. The neuroses include hysterias, obsessions, phobias, anxieties, among their commonest manifestations. They are what is called 'compromise formations', by-products of the conflict. I said above that the censorship allows elements from the unconscious into consciousness only on certain conditions. These require that the unconscious impulses or ideas must disguise themselves in various ways so that the conscious mind does not recognize them for what they are but accepts them in the assumed form, one normally acceptable to the standards of consciousness, or if not fully acceptable at least tolerated. In this way elements from the unconscious can mingle with the conscious system without being detected in their true nature. Thus a repressed sadistic impulse finding pleasure in inflicting cruelty may contribute to the enjoyment a surgeon gets in his work, but his conscious mind will attribute the pleasure to the fact that he is helping his fellowmen, or that he has done a clean and efficient piece of work.

When pressure from the unconscious is weak the so-called censorship is easily able to impose a complete disguise on the intruding element and the conscious mind will be quite unaware that there is an intruding element. But if the pressure is severe, the disguise is apt to be less complete and the com-promise formations, that is, the unconscious elements in their disguised form, cannot be so readily assimilated into the normal conscious behaviour. It is told of the great Dr Johnson that he felt an overpowering impulse as he walked along the street to strike with his cane every lamp-post he passed. He found this a most irrational and undignified habit and tried to overcome it. By force of will he on occasions would manage to pass one without striking it. But it was in vain, for a great uneasiness would thereupon descend on him, which he could only abate by returning to strike the missed post. This post-striking was undoubtedly a compromise formation. It is of an obsessional type that is fairly common. Its roots would be in his unconscious. His struggle against it showed that it was not a product of his conscious, reason-controlled behaviour. In other words, it was a minor neurosis. Such compromise forma-tions enter into the behaviour of every person, affecting his beliefs, judgements, feelings, actions. The extent depends upon the severity of the conflict. The difference between the normally healthy mind and the neurotic is simply one of degree, not of kind. The phobias, the obsessions, the sharp symptoms of the neurotic pass in their milder form in the ordinary person as moods, idiosyncrasies, mannerisms, peculiarities of temperament. In the healthy person some more or less plausible explanation of the oddities can usually be found, but when they are so strong as to constitute a neurosis only the plea of illness appears to explain them, and it is not an explanation but a description or restatement of the oddity.

It was not until Freud developed the technique and theory of psychoanalysis that neurotic symptoms were seen as compromise formations between unconscious impulses and the repressing forces protecting the conscious mind. Freud used psychoanalysis as a method of undoing the repression and making the hitherto unconscious elements accessible in their undisguised form to consciousness. That is, he brought them out of the unconscious into conciousness. This is no easy task, for the forces of repression set up an active resistance to every attempt to uncover what is in the unconscious and the resistance has to be overcome step by step. Like the repression the resistance is unconscious. In fact it is best understood as the repression continuing its effort to keep what is unconscious out of consciousness. The technique of psychoanalysis is devised to overcome the resistance and repression. In the measure that it succeeds the unconscious is opened up to consciousness and brought under its reasonable judgement. A new state of mind is brought about. When seen in the light of conscious standards of value the hitherto repressed ideas or impulses usually lose the terrifying aspect which they have had in the unconscious and which led to their repression. They can be assimilated to the conscious system without great difficulty and they no longer become a source of inner conflict to drain away the energy of the mind.

Perhaps this over-generalized description gives the impression that the repressing forces are localized, as it were, at one point in the mind or that there is an independent organ or instrument of repression and that psychoanalysis is a means of anaesthetizing or neutralizing it and thus setting free the contents of the unconscious as through a door propped open. Freud himself appears to have regarded it in this way at first, judging by his early use of hypnosis as a method of overcoming resistance and opening up the unconscious mind. He soon found, however, that the resistance was only driven further back and intensified at the new point. He discovered that there is no way of undoing repression at one blow, or even several blows. If anything it gathers strength as the psychoanalysis proceeds. At any rate the unconscious has to be uncovered piecemeal and resistance overcome on every bit of material that is brought from it to the light of consciousness. Psychoanalysis is a long and laborious process, requiring hard work on the part both of the patient and the psychoanalyst, and however long an analysis may go on – some have gone on for years – it is probable that there are still untouched depths of the unconscious to be explored. In clinical treatment the goal is to restore the patient to normal health, so it is rare for an analysis to be prolonged when this has been achieved.

The first answer to the question, 'What is psychoanalysis?', is, then, that it is a psychotherapeutic technique for treating neurotic disorders. But this is not a complete answer, as we have already seen, for the technique of psychoanalysis presupposes the validity of a theory or group of theories about the structure and functioning of the mind. Here, of course, we come upon more uncertain ground. The theory has to be based almost wholly on the material uncovered by applying the technique. This inevitably leaves room for different interpretations of the material and these are likely to shape the further developments of technique in the hands of different investigators. That is why there have sprung up different systems of so-called 'modern psychology', although all accept the basic ideas of the unconscious and repression, with which Freud began his work.

This book is not the place for a discussion of the relative merits of the different systems associated with the names of Freud, Jung, Adler, and the others. The writer believes that Freud and his school have made a more scientific, accurate and comprehensive contribution to the understanding of human behaviour than any other school of psychology and in the following pages the argument will take no account of what other schools have to say. The differences between them are far-reaching and they cannot be compared piecemeal. For the same reason it is quite inaccurate to lump them all together. That is to give up the hope of thinking seriously about them. Some years ago the President of the Psychological

Section of the British Medical Association pleaded that the name 'psychoanalysis' should be reserved for that system of theory and practice associated with Freud, and that other terms – and we may instance the 'deep analysis' of William Brown – should be found for other schools. It would avoid much confusion if this suggestion were generally adopted. It will be followed in this book.

Psychoanalysis, then, is the psychotherapeutic technique and the system of ideas developed by Freud and the Freudian school of psychology. It is correct to call it a psychology. Although psychoanalysis began as a method of treating neuroses and is still mostly used as such, it is too far-reaching to be confined within the limits of medical theory and practice. In the search to understand the causes of neurotic disorder Freud discovered psychological principles which are true of the normal healthy mind as well as of the disordered. The neuroses are products of the normal functions of the mind. They are not alien intruders into the mental system, having no laws, or separate laws of their own. They are abnormal in that they result from a disturbance in the normal balance of mental functioning, but they obey its laws. Just as the study of bodily disorders helps us to understand the healthy body, so the study of the neuroses throws great light on normal functioning of the mind. It serves rather like a microscope magnifying one item out of its normal proportion to the rest. No doubt much of the present knowledge gained through psychoanalysis needs to be supplemented or corrected by much more study of normal persons than has so far been possible, but already the basic structure and development of the mind has been made clear.

This takes us beyond the field of medicine into every study of human activity, and all our beliefs and practices in every field need to be re-examined in the light of the new knowledge. Whether it is in religion, ethics, anthropology, politics, or anything else, we start from implicit psychological theories, beliefs about the rationality of man, or his motives, or freedom, and so on, theories which we seldom pause to analyse because we have taken them over without reflection from current thought, or because they seem self-evident to us from our own conscious introspection. The revelation which psychoanalysis brings of the tremendous part played in our lives by our unconscious, and the further light thrown on conscious mentality, cannot but bring profound changes in our conceptions in every sphere of human behaviour. Not least is this true of religion and of Christianity in particular. For Christianity claims the allegiance of the whole man and aims to bring all his activities under its direction. More than any other religion it implies a theory of the nature of man. It is therefore a fit subject for psychoanalytical investigation.

CHAPTER 3

PSYCHOANALYSIS AS A DISCIPLINE

So far we have been using the terms 'conscious' and 'unconscious' in a general way and we need to define them more carefully.

It will be most convenient simply to adopt the current psychoanalytic terminology. (For a more detailed exposition, see Freud, *The Ego and the Id*, pp. 10ff.) There are three kinds of mental states. The term 'states' is not used in a static sense but has a dynamic significance as well; for any idea, memory, feeling, or aim of the mind is active. Mental states are conscious; or they are latent and capable of being called into consciousness; or they are repressed and cannot be called into consciousness. We shall use the term 'consciousness' or 'the conscious' for the first; 'the preconscious' for the second; and 'the unconscious' for the third. Strictly speaking we should use the terms as adjectives, describing mental states as conscious, preconscious, or unconscious (for which Freud adopts the symbols Cs, Pcs, Ucs), since the prefix 'the' seems to indicate areas of the mind, and this is misleading. Nevertheless, if we remember that the demarcation is not spatial or topographical, dividing the mind into areas of functioning, but simply distinguishes different kinds of functioning, it will be convenient to follow the usage I have suggested until it becomes necessary to introduce more exact terminology.

Let me illustrate what the terms mean. As I write I am conscious of the pencil I am using, of the paper before me, and of the thought I am trying to express in this sentence. I am also vaguely conscious of various other things, like noises coming from an adjoining room, the chair in which I am sitting, the outline of my thumb holding the paper steady, and so on. There is no clear margin of consciousness. Perceptions and ideas shade off gradually into nothingness. As I was writing I was not thinking of what I did after lunch today, but as I seek an illustration of a preconscious mental state my mind turns to some household repairs I then did. Before it came into consciousness this memory was in my preconscious, or was preconscious. When I turned my attention inwards, like a spotlight of the mind, as it were, it lit up the memory and made it conscious. There were many other memories available that might have become conscious. Indeed, many did and this one was selected from among them. But now I try to recall the name of a certain man whom I knew years ago, and knew well. The name eludes me. I have tried before to remember it and failed. The name is no longer available to my consciousness. What has happened to it? I say I have forgotten it. That only restates the fact that I cannot any longer recall it to consciousness. There are two possible explanations of this process of forgetting. One presumes that the name has passed out of my mind altogether and no longer exists in either consciousness or unconsciousness, like an impression worn away. The other explanation is that the memory exists in the mind, is unconscious, but is prevented from entering consciousness. Now there may be genuine forgetting in the sense of something really passing completely out of the mind and not merely out of consciousness; but if there is it is considerably less than is popularly supposed, as many experiments have shown. There is very much evidence that seems to point to the conclusion that nothing is lost to the mind and that every experience can under certain conditions be recalled. At any rate, whether this is so or not, it is certainly proved that very much of what is forgotten is simply stored in some part of the mind inaccessible to consciousness. It is repressed and therefore unconscious.

In the instance I have cited I know that I was once conscious of the name and I also am sure that I would recognize it immediately if it were mentioned to me. But psychoanalysis has shown that the unconscious also contains much of which we have no knowledge that it was ever present in our minds, things that our conscious mind would repudiate as unclean, evil, dangerous, absurd. And, as we have seen, the conscious mind is not just passively unable to reach these unconscious elements. A hostile barrier prevents them from becoming conscious; it also resists anything that may help them to do so.

We are not conscious of the barrier. We do not perceive that we are actively refusing to allow something into consciousness. The resistance is not therefore a deliberate, conscious act. It does not belong to the conscious system. There is no barrier between the conscious and the preconscious. It is true that the margin of the preconscious seems to fluctuate. When we are tired, for instance, we sometimes find it hard to remember things that would normally come readily to mind. But this fluctuation is on the far side, if we may for the moment continue the spatial metaphor, and is the border between the preconscious and the unconscious. It is there between the preconscious and the unconscious that the barrier lies and there seem to be some marginal elements which are now one side, now the other, of the barrier. But it is misleading to take spatial descriptions of mental functioning too literally. A better analogy is this. Attention is like a searchlight. Whatever we turn it to is, as it were, lit up by the beam, that is, it becomes conscious, is perceived. We may turn it outwards to objects or inwards to ideas, feelings, memories, the whole content of the mind. Whatever is lit up by this inward perception becomes conscious and whatever can thus become conscious belongs to the preconscious system. Whenever the searchlight is turned towards something belonging to the unconscious, the beam is switched off, but we do not know that it is switched off. Nothing is lit up and we do not realize that there was anything there for us to see.

We can therefore treat consciousness as a special aspect of the preconscious system. It is that part of it which is being perceived at the moment, and for the sake of convenience we can lump both together under the one term consciousness, using it to denote the whole system of mental processes of which we can readily become conscious. Having noted the difference between conscious and preconscious we can put it aside except when for special reasons it is necessary to emphasize that at the moment an idea is or is not in consciousness, in the narrower sense of the term.

The resistance which divides consciousness (Cs plus Pcs)

from the unconscious creates a serious difficulty for anyone who is trying to analyse the ways in which the unconscious enters into and helps to shape the feelings, beliefs, ideals, actions and so on that constitute religious behaviour, or any other field of human life. To be able to do this he requires some knowledge of psychoanalysis, which consists very largely of the study of unconscious mental processes by its special techniques. This in turn means that he must study his own unconscious mind and it is precisely here that the difficulty arises. Deliberate, reasoned thinking, which we must use when we attempt such a study, is a function of consciousness. Because the unconscious is excluded from consciousness we cannot directly observe our own unconscious mental processes. They work according to different laws and cannot enter consciousness in their own form and they are also kept out by the barrier of resistance, resistance of which we are quite unaware. Particularly does this barrier operate when it is not merely a question of considering general tendencies but one of unveiling the actual ideas and impulses which we have repressed. We may give intellectual acceptance to the idea that we have an unconscious and that it is dynamic, influencing our behaviour, but the mere idea that our unconscious exists is itself part of consciousness and it does not carry with it the ability to perceive directly what is in that unconscious. Belief in the unconscious is not enough to overcome the repressions which maintain it.

The resistance against the recognition of the contents of our own unconscious mind also works in a large measure to debar us from perceiving the same kind of thing in anything with which we are in some way identified, our own nation, for instance, or our religious faith. We only recognise the traits resembling our repressions in some external object when we can condemn them, thus giving our resistance a further opportunity to express itself. We frequently read into other people by a process of projection the very character-istics of our own unconscious, and because we do so fail to observe them correctly, like the angry man who imagines that he is keeping cool and it is the others who are getting hot and bothered. The operation of the resistance distorts our thinking about the outside world as well as about ourselves.

Religion is a field in which the unconscious finds many ways of expression. If we are to appreciate the extent to which this is so we need to take full account of the working in ourselves of this unconscious resistance and do so not as an afterthought to allow for a margin of error in our thinking, but by putting it into the forefront. Otherwise we shall rely on introspection alone and be arguing in a circle. When, for instance, we try to analyse the factors which contribute to shaping our idea of God, introspection gives us only the conscious reasons for this belief and conceals from us the part played by the unconscious elements. It therefore seems to us that our belief is entirely rational and justified by the reasons we adduce and we are convinced that no other explanation is needed. We resist and even resent any suggestion to the contrary. It is true that in observing the behaviour of other people we often suspect them of irrationality, and the reasons they give for their beliefs and conduct may appear to us inadequate to explain or justify them, but so far as we ourselves are concerned introspection always convinces us that our reasons are sound. When in this field or in any other our attention is forced to something which is in fact largely determined by the unconscious, we go to all manner of lengths to provide what seems to us an adequate explanation or else we strenuously dodge the point. Such false explanations are known as 'rationalizations'. They are conscious reasons devised to explain some element of behaviour which has its origin in the unconscious, and they serve the purpose of protecting us from recognizing the unconscious origin.

No one is exempt from the danger of being led astray by his own unconscious. Every student of psychoanalysis, from the beginner to the most advanced, needs to remind himself that it is more than a set of ideas to be played with as so many counters. It is primarily a technique for opening up the mind and it achieves its result by altering the dynamic balance of forces in the mind so as to secure release of the repressed elements. As such it has proved of immense value in treating certain types of deranged minds, but it can be applied to more normal minds with equal penetration and parallel results. It always changes the mind. It is not just a set of ideas to be understood. It is a treatment to apply to the mind and can only be understood in so far as it is thus applied. It is true, as we have seen, that the use of psychoanalysis has led to the discovery of a series of facts about the functioning of the mind and to the formulation of certain theories which are grouped under the name psychoanalysis. The student is under a constant pressure from his resistance to think of psycho-analysis as merely a body of knowledge and theories and to forget that it is a method of changing the mind. Such an over-simplification debars us from understanding our own minds and the work of psychoanalysis and also, of course, falsifies our attempts to apply it to the explanation of other fields of human life.

To understand what is necessary we should take note of clinical practice. In the analysis of a patient the psychoanalyst concentrates directly upon overcoming the resistance as the means of securing the release of the repressions which he is aiming at. He may have been able to deduce in advance the nature of these repressions but he makes no progress at all by telling the patient what they are, that he is repressing this or that impulse or memory. The patient may be prepared to believe him, though usually he resists, but there is no effective gain. That only comes when the resistance is overcome and the patient is able to perceive for himself and not merely believe that he had actually been entertaining the ideas in question.

In reading a book like this one the reader has no one to assist him to overcome his unconscious resistance (and he must not be led astray into thinking he has none) in the way the analyst helps his patient, but he must come to terms with it if he wants to advance to a real understanding of what truth there is in the ideas put forward in it. This must be stressed again and again. The resistance works in innumerable ways. One of the commonest is by drawing attention away from itself and leading the student to forget his own resistance. He should try to make it a routine procedure to check his thinking at frequent intervals to look for signs of its working.

Strong repressions make us hostile towards theories which depend for their proof on bringing the repressed element into the open. The violent abuse which psychoanalysis first met and the heat with which some of its theories are still received is an instance of this. So is the contemptuous dismissal of psychoanalysis that some critics affect. The student is exposed to the danger that his resistance will make him dismiss the arguments as absurd without giving them much consideration. By pooh-poohing them he succeeds in evading the need to face up to his own unconscious. Perhaps I should add that there is a danger of accepting psychoanalytic ideas too readily, for this is another way of achieving the same evasion, but a more subtle one. If you already accept psychoanalysis there is no need to examine the evidence further, for you must have already done so fully to be convinced of its truth. Therefore you do not have to dig any deeper into the unconscious. Many people who talk a lot about psychoanalysis and their 'complexes' are in fact doing so as a means of running away from their real repressions, while at the same time getting unconscious pleasure out of giving them disguised expression. They are using the double bluff on themselves. But a sound knowledge of psychoanalysis requires that the student face up to his own resistances and repressions – that he get to know the contents of his own unconscious.

The student of psychoanalysis then, is required not merely to exercise his logical reasoning upon a series of given facts, as he would be if he were studying, say, physics. Something more is necessary to help him reach the truth. In physics the influence of the unconscious can on the whole be neglected, though not entirely. Not so when we are studying human motives and interests. In this field we have to take account of the distortions of thought due to the conflict between the conscious and the unconscious. The only way to correct the distortions is by resolving the conflict in ourselves, that is, by overcoming our repressions and opening up our minds. Unless we do so we cannot properly assess the facts we are trying to study. This means that to undertake a psychoanalytic study is to undergo a discipline of the mind in which we set free forces held imprisoned or fixed in our conflicts. When the conflict is resolved our mental growth can continue. With every step that reduces inner mental conflict the whole personality is strengthened and achieves greater integration and freedom. In this psycho-analysis is like Christianity, which also gives strength and unity and inner freedom. We shall say more about this at a later point.

This warning is all the more necessary in this book, in which no attempt will be made to justify the psychoanalytic theories put forward. It should be borne in mind most care-fully throughout. In what follows I am only trying to explain psychoanalytic theory. The reader will therefore find certain ideas set out and will not be taken through the steps of testing and sifting the evidence. Had he to do so he would be thereby encouraged to take upon himself the discipline necessary to get some knowledge of his own unconscious and come to terms with it. If he is to take advantage of what psychoanalysis has discovered he must attempt the discipline at some stage.

The human mind has been likened to an iceberg with one-tenth able to enter into consciousness and nine-tenths sub-merged in the unconscious. We cannot be exact about pro-portions, nor does the ratio remain constant throughout the life of the individual, but the analogy conveys a large measure of truth. We must also remember that there are not two minds, one conscious and the other unconscious, but that there is one mind of which the conscious and the unconscious are both functions. Further, the unconscious is extremely active, constantly striving to pass through consciousness to the normal channels of expression. These are speech, gesture, action, all the means whereby mental striving is translated into physical form and can be used to act upon the environ-ment. We shall therefore expect the unconscious to enter largely into all our mental processes, even though we do not perceive it directly, and we should be on the watch to detect the signs of its presence.

It is sometimes said that Christianity has always had its own form of psychoanalysis in the practice of confession. This is a very misleading statement, for confession and psychoanalysis are quite different. Confession has considerable psychological as well as moral value but it must not be confused with psychoanalysis. It deals only with conscious processes of the mind and calls upon the use of the will to combat moral failings. It is true that a skilled confessor will compel the penitent to examine his mind more carefully and honestly than he has been doing, but he still works only on the conscious level. The psychoanalyst, on the other hand, tries to pierce through the conscious level to penetrate and expose the unconscious, and he works chiefly there. He does not call on the patient's willpower, but endeavours to get him to relax, making much more use of the patient's imagination. Further, he is not concerned with passing moral judgements on his patient's behaviour or, at any rate directly, with strengthening him morally. He aims at resolving the inner psychological conflicts which have caused the illness and is content to cure the latter. That as a result of this the patient should develop greater moral strength as well is part of the way the human mind is made up. The psychoanalyst, however, cannot aim at it directly. He tries to clear away the rubbish that is choking the spring of life and is not concerned with what happens to the stream when he has restored the flow. The confessor on the other hand is pre-occupied with directing the flow into the right channels. Thus they are engaged on quite different tasks. Both may be necessary, but the value of the confessor should not blind us to the need of the work of the psychoanalyst.

CHAPTER 4

INSTINCT, SUBLIMATION AND CULTURE

THE psychological sources of cultural activities, including religion, are the instincts. The instincts are the driving power of the mind, the sources of its energy. Without them it would not work at all. The repressed elements as well as the forces which repress them draw their energy from the instincts. From the simplest image or idea floating in the mind to the great inclusive purposes sustained over a lifetime, there is nothing which does not depend on this source for activation.

The study of the instincts in man, their nature, functions, metamorphoses and developments is one of the most difficult tasks of psychology. It is an essential part of Freudian psychoanalysis. It was for his theory of the instincts that Freud was from the beginning most bitterly attacked, particularly for his analysis of the structure and development of the sex instinct.

Instinct and intelligence are sometimes contrasted as opposing or alternative forms of conduct. This is misleading, for it treats instinct as a quasi-automatic mode of behaviour, such as we seem to see in certain forms of insect life. But close study of these forms has shown that even in the most rigid types of instinct – in wasps, bees, ants, termites, spiders, etc. – there is scope for initiative and variation, the exercise of which is intelligence, however rudimentary. On the other hand the ambitious man, spending years of thought and effort to attain success, or the scientist devoting a lifetime to the pursuit of knowledge, or the saint living a life of self-sacrifice, is fulfilling the urge of his instincts. The instincts use the intelligence to secure their ends and the intelligence directs and co-ordinates the instinctive drives. They are different aspects of mental processes and do not function separately in man. Certainly an instinctive drive of some sort enters into every bit of mental activity. The real contrast is not between instinct and intelligence, but between modes of instinctive behaviour which are fixed in their form of expression, allowing very little scope for modification and adaptation to changes of circumstances, and those in which the form of expression is not closely determined, allowing a wide variety of behaviour in pursuit of the same general goal. In the latter the ultimate expression of the instinct may be so far removed from its primitive source that the connexion is at first sight unrecognizable. In such cases there is usually no set form of instinctive action predetermined by the constitution. There is only a general pattern of behaviour which takes on particular forms of expression according to circumstances and accumulated experience. This leaves enormous scope in one individual for an instinct to manifest itself in a multitude of ways, and for the habits of thought and conduct formed in this way from the same instinct to differ very much from individual to individual. It leaves room, too, for intelligence to be applied in selecting ways of expressing the instinctive urge, both in the action of the moment and in the formation of habits.

It follows that when we observe instincts in man it is in the form that they have developed in the course of the individual's growth, that is, we see them as behaviour habits acquired through experience. In man, also, the instincts are not rigidly separated from each other but easily intermingle and combine. It is therefore a mistake to try to differentiate a large number of sharply defined instincts, as some psychologists, notably William McDougall, have done. Instead we should observe the broad general patterns of instinctive behaviour.

There are three main groupings, within each of which we find component or subordinate instincts. These three are the sex instincts, the ego instincts, and the aggressive instincts. Of these the most complicated is the sex instinct (or instincts) and the study of it is rendered still more difficult because it is most subject to repression.

It is wrong to speak of an instinct of religion or an instinct of worship. Religious behaviour has an instinctive basis but it is not itself a primary instinct. Were it so we should be able to trace its counterpart in the lower forms of animal life, where it would be even more clearly defined than in man.

It is a derivative of the more primitive instincts, chiefly, in fact, of the sexual instincts. Later in this book we shall be tracing some of the main lines of this derivation.

Religion is not alone in this. All our culture and civilization is similarly built on the foundation of the primitive instincts. By denying them outlet at the primitive level, reserves of energy are created which in the course of history man has used to build up civilization with all its complexities and refinements. The education of the individual, which trains him to membership of civilization, requires that the instinctive urges be diverted from primitive satisfactions to those prescribed by culture and civilization, so that he becomes adapted to his social environment.

This diversion of primitive instinctive urges to more remote ends takes place through the operation of certain psychological mechanisms of which repression is one of the most important in its consequences. In subsequent chapters we shall see the part played in this process by particular instinct-formations, such as the Oedipus Complex. Let us here examine some of the general characteristics of instinct-diversion. It is important to recognize them before we proceed to a detailed analysis of them.

Man has inherited his instincts from his brute ancestry. The difference between instincts in man and in the lower animals simply is, as we have seen, that in man they are more flexible, less fixed in the forms of actions which they prompt, more capable of education through experience to new kinds of action, and as a result vastly more complex and less easily identifiable. Man cannot behave as an animal for the simple reason that his instincts are constitutionally more plastic and require the mould of experience to give them set forms, such as, for instance, in the manifestations of love and the objects which the sex instincts seek. This capacity of the instincts to learn by experience is part result part cause of raising man above the animals. Man is the heir to the development of his ancestors, human and brute, through the unknown ages.

This flexibility of the developing instincts in man is a necessary condition of the greatly increased intelligence of man. What man has lost through the growing diffuseness of his instinctive reactions he has more than gained by the development of his intelligence as an instrument in directing his behaviour. His intelligence enables him to see alternative modes of action and to foresee their possible consequences. It makes for richer satisfaction of his needs and greatly enlarges the possible range of action. It has enabled him to employ tools and to subdue the forces of nature to his ends. None of this would have been possible if he had been tied by his innate constitution to rigid, almost unvarying modes of behaviour.

For man to reach this combination of instinct and intelligence he needs a long period of growing up. In the early part of it his instincts are unfolding and reach out, as it were, towards the world on which they will ultimately express themselves in the actions that will bring satisfaction. They take shape according to the nature of the experience of the infant. This early period, the first five years of life, is the most vital in shaping the personality, for in it the instincts are in their most plastic state and their subsequent development can be profoundly affected by what happens to the infant. The following years bring the unfolding of the earlier patterns as the experience of the child widens and as his intelligence is fostered by education and by the sheer necessity of dealing with more complex situations than those of infancy. As he grows up the great general goals of life are formed, a body of knowledge is acquired which enables the intelligence to make its choices more effectively, and the personality becomes set.

If we were able from the beginning of our lives to get primitive satisfactions for our instinctive urges, we should not rise very far above the animal level. Hunger or sexual desire, for instance, that found immediate satisfaction, would expend itself immediately and never prompt to more remote forms of action, such as those required by the infinitely complex economic system in which civilized man lives. But man does not find primitive satisfactions ready to hand. All sorts of barriers come between the urge and the satisfaction. One instinct may clash with another. For example, fear may prevent us taking the food that someone else has, however hungry we are. And if there is no food at hand to gratify our hunger we must needs postpone satisfaction. Society imposes all sorts of restrictions on gratification – it forbids us to steal, to murder, to rape – and if need be it enforces its commands physically. Finally, we build up an ideal of conduct, an ego-ideal, by which we ourselves restrain our own primitive instincts through the power exercised by another part of ourselves.

All of these forms of restraint are conscious. Repression, which is one of the most potent forms of instinct restraint, is unconscious in its operation. It is related to the other forms but it has certain important differences which make its effects on the mind more disruptive and far-reaching. When repression debars instincts from getting direct expression, the consequences may differ considerably from those which follow upon conscious restraint, particularly that which we deliberately impose on ourselves for the sake of an ideal of conduct that we have set up.

In real life we usually find some degree of intermingling of the different kinds of instinct frustration, so that while we may draw distinctions between them for the sake of analysis this does not mean that they necessarily function apart. But if we bear this in mind we can note the different ways of dealing with them.

First then, frustration through circumstances. If primitive man was hungry and could not find an animal to slay, he was quickened to greater efforts in his hunting or had to turn to fruits and other vegetable substitutes. Frustration compelled him to think and plan how to find food to satisfy his hunger. Over the ages necessity in this way compelled man to learn how to procure food efficiently, how to store it, how to grow it. Out of the frustrations of first primitive appetites grew up the vast world-wide network of the modern economic system. Unsatisfied hunger is a great teacher.

The frustrations imposed by society provoke somewhat different reactions. The violence of the unsatisfied instinct may be so great as to lead to rebellion against society, either open or clandestine. By such behaviour the rebel forfeits his fellowship in the society and risks the condemnation and punishment by which the social code is sanctioned. If, however, he accepts the prohibition he must find substitute ways of satisfying his instinct, fresh outlets for his energy. The code which forbade one line of action may possibly suggest an alternative, e.g. work instead of theft, or it may impose conditions under which the first instinctive impulse is permissible, e.g. marriage instead of indiscriminate sexual indulgence. All the instincts come under the ban of society in one way or another, constraining them to seek satisfaction in certain clearly defined ways or else to seek substitute satisfactions which do not evoke social disapproval. Work and play and art are some of the ways in which frustrated instincts can find at least some expression. Education largely consists in training the instinctive tendencies to accept the restrictions and to find socially acceptable outlets in other pursuits. The growth of civilization is the education of the race.

The frustrations imposed by an individual upon himself because of an ideal of conduct are not so easy to interpret since it requires a full knowledge of the structure of the mind, a very intricate and difficult topic. We shall examine it more fully at a later stage when we shall see that the ego-ideal is part of something we call the Super-ego, a part of the mind which arrogates to itself the right to supervise the rest. It is, however, in this sphere that the element of moral judgement enters. Morality depends on self-control, the recognition and pursuit of an ideal of conduct by which the instinctive impulses are tested and allowed or forbidden according to whether they conform or not to the ideal. The power used by the Super-ego in the service of the ego-ideal to control the instincts is itself drawn from the instincts during the formative period of the child's life, and the process by which this takes place links the ego-ideal very closely with religion.

When an instinctive tendency or impulse is frustrated by the Super-ego it is usually necessary to find substitute gratifications. The Super-ego is unconditional in its demands. It is the seat of the 'categorical imperative', the unyielding 'ought' of morality. The capacity to find substitute gratifications depends on a number of factors – the severity of the Super-ego, the nature of the instinctive energies it has been able to capture in its service, the degree to which it is susceptible to reason, and, most important of all and closely interwoven with the other factors, the extent to which it operates unconsciously concurrently with its conscious vetoes. For the unconscious operation of the Super-ego is the source of repression, and, as we saw, repression is one of the most potent factors in instinct prohibition. When repression causes the frustration the process of finding the necessary substitute satisfactions passes out of conscious direction and the range of substitutes is infinitely widened because of the character of the unconscious.

We can picture mental activity in this way. When an impulse is stirred up it is as if an amount of energy is liberated from its storehouse, creating tension or pressure along a given channel or set of channels. If the energy is allowed to flow freely along the channel it is converted into action. This works off the tension and brings satisfaction. There is quiescence until further energy is released. Satisfaction and release of tension come through discharge in action. Consciousness controls the organs of expression – speech, gesture, actions, all the means by which the individual carries his impulses and purposes into action upon the environment in the effort to satisfy them. The unconscious, that is, the repressed, is denied direct expression of this sort. It cannot get the satisfaction of release of tension along the appropriate channels.

Let us follow the stages more closely. Some stimulus starts an impulse in the depths of the mind and thus sets energy free. It tries to flow along the channels by which it would normally get discharge in action and so achieve the proper satisfaction. Because of repression it finds the channel blocked. At a certain level the released energy comes up against the repressing force, which bars its entry into consciousness and to the organs of action. The result is extremely significant. The energy of the impulse cannot now be set free unless it can find some other channels to get discharge. We can imagine it therefore being dammed up by the repressing force until the tension is so great that it turns back upon its tracks and creates pressure in a new direction, like a stream coming up against a closed floodgate. It continues to exert its forward pressure against the barrier of repression and it can only be contained by a force at least equal to itself, put out by the repressing elements. The result may be a deadlock in which the repressed impulse is completely held in check by the repression. The tension cannot be released and in consequence there is a double loss of energy to the whole mind, of which repressed and repressing are parts. The undischarged energy of the repressed impulse locks up the energy required to hold it. If, therefore, repressions are severe, and no safety valves are permitted, the result may be to tie up so much mental energy in the internal unconscious conflict of repressed and repressing that the person involved is in a continual state of mental exhaustion.

As a rule repression is not as severe as this. The repressed impulse, after being held up by the barrier of repression, is able to find side-channels of expression, subject to various conditions. A kind of compromise is reached. The impulse, for instance, may pass into action which consciousness does not perceive, such as an unconscious gesture or a facial twitch. Such unconscious actions can very rarely be considered as normal satisfactions of the impulse. In severe cases we get the phenomenon known as 'fugue', a form of mental illness in which the sufferer is liable to periods of loss of memory and even to changes of personality, during which he may behave to all appearances like a normal man but in a different personality from his ordinary self, a personality possessing its own identity, memories, ideas, purposes. During these periods of 'absence' he has no knowledge of his normal life and in his normal life he has no recollection of anything he did in them. The connexions in the mind are almost certainly there, but they are repressed and are only recoverable as a rule under psychotherapeutic treatment.

There are other ways in which unconscious impulses gain fairly direct access to the organs of expression and lead to action of which consciousness remains unaware. In all of them the repression partially fails at the earlier level but maintains itself at the level of action by keeping the action unconscious. This kind of manifestation of the activity of the unconscious is interesting from the general psychological point of view or for psychotherapeutics, but it is not directly important for the study of the contribution of the unconscious to religion. We find the richest material for this in some of the other manifestations of the unconscious.

We are tracing what happens to an impulse in the unconscious which is striving to pass through consciousness into action, but which has come up against the repressing forces of the mind before it can enter consciousness. So far we have noted that a deadlock may be reached, immobilizing a double quantity of energy, or else the impulse may attain to action that is dissociated or split off from the main personality and so remains unconscious to it. Another way of satisfaction is possible by which the unconscious and the repressing force come to an agreement on a middle path.

We have likened the stimulation of the impulse to the release from the storehouse of the mind of a charge of energy which, once released, cannot be put back but goes on searching for a way into action, its ordinary outlet. Meeting the barrier of repression the energy of the impulse turns back and flows under the pressure into side-channels which represent other similar lines of action or connect with them. In one of these it finds a way that does not arouse the hostility of the repressing force and it can flow along this channel to satisfaction by discharge in action. It takes on the form of the new action. It no longer appears in its original form but emerges into consciousness as though it were the normal impulse of the secondary channel and nothing else. In other words, the repressed impulse has taken on a disguise and by doing so has made itself acceptable to consciousness.

We must not take the physical metaphor of the channel too strictly. It seems certain that no transference of energy from one impulse to another can take place without actual links in the nervous structure, but the study of such transferences of energy, or displacement, as this psychological mechanism is called, offers more promise on the psychological level. The unconscious is extremely rich in its capacity for displacement. One reason for this is that the unconscious does not think logically, but in pictures and by associations of every kind – shape, colour, sound, contiguity, function, and so on – and can also use the most trivial connexions as a bridge from one idea to another and as a means of displacing the energy of one impulse into the form of another. For instance, in the unconscious two people may be associated because of the colour of their eyes, or because they have the same Christian name, or both have spaniel dogs. There is no limit to the fertility of the unconscious in making such displacements. Once the connexion is established, it does not carry only those things which might seem to bear on it, but it is used to carry a whole mass of material that is quite irrelevant to the connecting link.

A man jilted by a girl in circumstances that made him feel greatly humiliated, came in course of time to cease feeling resentful about her and even to forget her for long periods. But he developed a strong dislike for a certain town which he could not explain by any adequate reasons. It was the town where he had first met the girl, but he had forgotten that. He had unconsciously transferred his resentment against the girl to the town which he associated with her, also unconsciously.

The psychological term 'displacement' is used to describe the transfer of the energy charge of a repressed impulse to an associated idea by means of which it gains a disguised secondary satisfaction. It is applied to all forms of secondary expression and it therefore includes the symptoms of various psychoneurotic disorders such as hysterias and obsessional neuroses. These symptoms are compromise formations, compromises between the repressing force and the repressed impulse. When, however, the secondary form is not merely permitted but approved as desirable on social and moral grounds the displacement is sometimes called a 'sublimation'. That is the frequent and perhaps most popular meaning given to the term 'sublimation'. An instance of such sublimation would be the case of a woman who has no children of her own

47

and satisfies a strong maternal instinct by taking up work as a nurse, teacher, or social welfare worker. Or perhaps a man with a strong fear of his father 'sublimates' it into fear of God. Sublimation is a popular prescription with moralisers and is sometimes offered almost as a panacea for every difficulty in moral conduct.

According to this popular interpretation, sublimation is simply a displacement to a form socially and morally approved. The strictly psychological view is different and we should carefully note the difference because it has an important bearing on the analysis and interpretation of religious behaviour. Moral judgement as such is no concern of psychology. The act of making a moral judgement is a psychological phenomenon but the moral quality of the judgement, its rightness or wrongness, belongs to the sphere of ethics, not psychology. Hence the popular use of 'sublimation' mixes psychological and ethical standards and only confuses the issue. If we are to use it as a psychological term – and that is its proper sphere – it should be kept free of moral implications. In psychology it describes those instances of displacement which end in the secondary channel becoming transformed into a primary one.

Sublimation in this sense begins first as displacement following the repression of an impulse in the unconscious. In the usual way the primary impulse under repression seeks and finds another mode of expression which serves to give satisfaction whenever the impulse is stimulated. The displacement to the secondary satisfaction becomes a sublimation when the energy of the primary impulse undergoes a kind of short-circuit so that it flows directly into the secondary channel instead of attempting to find its outlet in the primary. Why this short-circuit should take place and under what conditions it does so are questions extremely difficult to answer, but it would seem that one reason is that the secondary channel gives a more complete and thorough satisfaction than the primary offers, and possibly also because the channel of sublimation provides satisfactions for a number of impulses which combine to make it a strong one, drawing the released energy of the mind directly to itself. The new satisfaction must also bear some resemblance to the forsaken primitive one, e.g. sport for murder. Once the sublimation is established little energy is needed to maintain repression of the impulse since it no longer seeks the forbidden channel. Mental conflict is reduced to a minimum and there is therefore a greater sum total of energy available to flow freely into action.

We may summarize it briefly this way. A repressed impulse is in bondage and also takes up an equal amount of energy to tie it down. The sublimated impulse is set free by its transformation and sets free also the repressing force. A mere displacement, that is, one that has not become a sublimation, is still under the pressure of repression, for it continually seeks to get satisfaction in the primary repressed way, and would revert to it if repression were removed. Hence displacement does not release all the energy tied up by conflict. A sublimation is not to be distinguished from a displacement by its moral quality or its adaptation to social standards, since a mere displacement may take this form. A life of self-sacrifice, for example, may be the expression of a free and highly developed personality; on the other hand, it may be the outcome of a strongly repressed masochism – a tendency or impulse to seek suffering because of the unconscious pleasure which is derived from it, and which is neurotic when strongly developed. It is no doubt much to be preferred that a strong repressed tendency or group of related unconscious impulses more or less constantly active – for which we may use the familiar term 'complex' – should find its displaced expression in conduct that is socially useful and morally praiseworthy, than in some useless or even burdensome way such as by sickness, which is a common enough outlet. Nevertheless, such a displaced expression, though superficially satisfactory, still retains its character as a product of the unconscious. It thereby differs from a true sublimation, which, though it may have originated as a result of repression, has grown free of it and lost the marks of its origin in the unconscious. It is almost always good in the moral sense, but it is good because it is a sublimation, not a sublimation because it is good.

It is important to distinguish between sublimation and displacement in the psychological study of religious behaviour, for there possibly is no field of thought and action where we can be so readily deceived about the nature of motives. Religion is a happy hunting ground for displacements – repressions finding a compromise expression in disguise. If we were to neglect the psychological criteria and treat as a sublimation any activity that had social approval we should certainly be in danger of getting ourselves into the position of calling Jesus a neurotic, or at least a crank, since the society of his day united to put him to death for the views he taught and the things he did; while on the other hand, we would be classing as healthy the actions of those who tortured and burnt in the name of religion, for these were highly approved in their day by their contemporaries. Our characters and our actions must certainly be measured by an objective standard, for good intentions are unreliable as a test of soundness, but conformity with the average opinion of our fellows is not a safe measuring rod. Every advance in thought and morals is an act of rebellion against prevailing standards and tends to be condemned.

It is easier to say that there must be a standard or norm of conduct than to determine what it is. We can only discover gradually what it is. It must remain as an ideal that always recedes as we approach it, for each gain reveals further heights beyond. To believe in the existence of such a norm of human development implies that there are absolute values which constitute perfection. Most people agree that goodness, truth and beauty are part of that norm, though they may differ about the meaning of them. The Christian sets Jesus as the pattern of perfection of human character but behind him, or revealed in him, they see the will of God for man. So far as I understand Christian teaching I believe that the perfect life will show its perfection by its truthfulness, its freedom, and its capacity to love, and anyone possessing these qualities is filled with power or creative energy.

These qualities can be simulated or they can be estimated on a false scale. We need as many checks on them as possible.

Psychoanalysis contributes one such check by the way it widens the conception of human action to include the unconscious as well as the conscious. It has enabled us to see that consciously we may be serving God and unconsciously following the precepts of the devil. Conscious and unconscious are integral parts of the whole man. It is not enough therefore to put on the surface mask of righteousness. We must have deeper harmony than that. That is why in studying religion we need to distinguish what is a real sublimation from a displacement, for in the latter we find, as it were, wolves masquerading in sheep's clothing. In a sublimation, however, the whole body is 'full of light'.

CHAPTER 5

THE STAGES OF DEVELOPMENT

WE can now turn from the general principles which have
so far been occupying our attention and concern ourselves
with some of the more specific discoveries of psychoanalysis.
If we were launched upon a straightforward study of psychoanalysis the best way of coming to terms with it would be to
retrace some of the early steps and see what evidence Freud
had on which to base his conclusions, how the evidence was
gathered and how the body of evidence and theory expanded.
In other words we would undertake a study of the unconscious
mind, and the student who wants to get a real grasp of the
subject is urged to do this. Freud once called psychoanalysis
'the science of unconscious mental processes'. The early
work of psychoanalysis was devoted to exploring the nature
and contents of the unconscious. The repressing forces, which
prevent the repressed mental processes from entering
consciousness, were vaguely classified as 'the ego-instincts'
and the core of them was noted as an 'ego-ideal'. Their function
was seen to be to protect the ego, the conscious self, from the
intrusions of those ideas and impulses which seemed objectionable to its standards or which endangered its control. It was
not until the structure, contents and modes of functioning of
the unconscious had been thoroughly explored that psychoanalysis extended its systematic mapping process to these
ego instincts, and so provided a picture of the whole mind.
This was given by Freud in *The Ego and the Id*, which appeared
in German in 1924, and which is one of the most important
books on psychology ever written. A thorough grasp of it is
essential to the understanding of psychoanalysis.

Our purpose in this book is a more limited one, to examine
the bearing of psychoanalysis on the Christian religion and to
indicate to the student of both some lines of thought which
the writer thinks are worth following up. Hence we will
content ourselves with presenting the main conclusions

reached by psychoanalysis without marshalling the evidence in support of them or reviewing the stages by which they were reached. But adopting this method makes it very necessary to repeat the warning that the student must come to terms with his own unconscious before he can hope to grasp their full significance.

The human mind is not fully developed at birth. Nor is the mind of the new-born infant just an immature version of the conscious mind of the adult; it follows different laws. The adult mind is the result of growth in which heredity and environment combine to produce the final form of the developed mind, both in its conscious and unconscious aspects. Heredity, which differs from individual to individual, comprises the instincts and abilities which in general are characteristic of the human species, such as the instincts of self-preservation and the ability to use the organs of sense perception. There seems no reason to doubt that individuals vary in the relative balance of strength in their instinctive endowment and that weaknesses (potential at any rate) can be inherited in the constitution. It does not follow that we should ascribe a manifested failing such as confirmed drunkenness to an inherited tendency to drink, even though such a failing may run in the family. It may be a kind of psychological infection passed from one person to another, a social inheritance through environment rather than an innate constitutional inheritance.

Heredity is the equipment with which nature endows the organism to maintain and propagate life in the world of real things and the ways in which the instincts operate will therefore be partly determined by the vicissitudes of circumstance. As the human instincts are much more plastic than those in the lower animals, less predetermined in their forms of expression, the experiences which the growing mind encounters can impress upon them an infinite multitude of ways of expressing themselves. Thus while the instincts in all men develop through certain phases, following the inner laws of native constitution, and while, too, there may be a general resemblance between the ways in which two different people may behave or between two different forms of behaviour in one person prompted by the one instinct, it is true to say that we can fully understand any mind only in the light of its history. The soundest method of psychology is to study mental growth. That is what we shall try to do.

First let us glance at the whole pattern of growth. From birth to death the human mind passes through many stages of development. We may classify them into six, and thereby amend the seven ages of man that Shakespeare gives, though the number could be increased by sub-divisions. The six stages are: (I) infancy, up to about six to seven years of age; (II) childhood, from seven to about twelve to thirteen; (III) adolescence, from thirteen to twenty to twenty-one; (IV) adulthood, from twenty-one to middle age; (V) middle age to old age; (VI) senescence, when the mental and physical functions degenerate; ending in death.

Of the six stages infancy is incomparably the most important psychologically, for it is in that period that the structure of the mind is fixed and the main lines of subsequent development laid down. It is a period of rapid growth and kaleidoscopic changes. The child begins it as a bundle of potentialities undeveloped, unco-ordinated, sub-personal. He emerges from it a complete person, thinking, feeling, willing in a co-ordinated way. His sex instincts have passed through three or four changes and become compounded into a central form; he has come to grips with the real world and established strong attachments to it; he has amassed a body of knowledge from experience; he has developed a strong and active ego and has learnt how to be a member of society; and he has developed an organ of conscience and self-control to set standards and values to direct his behaviour. Some of these may be relatively weak, but they have taken on their characteristic shape and will not undergo further profound modifications. Even the basis of his personal character has been fixed permanently. The subsequent stages of development will simply build upon the foundations laid in infancy, develop the tendencies formed then. Infancy is the main period of the structural growth of the mind.

This stage comes to its end with the resolution of the Oedipus Complex. We shall return to that later. The stage of childhood which follows it is a period of latency in which the sexual instincts cease to undergo violent changes. Their energy, or libido as it is termed, becomes as it were desexualized or 'aim-inhibited' and shows itself in general activity and enables the child to consolidate the mental structure attained in infancy and put it to the test of living. It is as though infancy were the period of growing up and childhood a kind of first adulthood. Certainly in childhood the psyche is tough and strong and free from the emotional storms which characterize the stages of growth. If it is not it is a sign that the child has not properly passed through the stages of infancy, but is caught in one of them, in a state of 'fixation'.

The stage of childhood comes to an end with the onset of puberty and adolescence. This is another period of growth and instability, a second infancy. It is not so profound as the first infancy. In it the latency period of desexualization ends and the early stages of development are briefly recapitulated and then the sexual instinct (it is now more correct to use the singular) enters its final stage and becomes fully mature. The rest of the personality develops with it and prepares the individual for adulthood and its responsibilities as an independent member of a society, as a partner in marriage and as a parent.

Each of the stages has its own interesting features and much has been written about them, particularly the early stages. From the psychological point of view there is room for much more careful study of the specific characteristics of the fifth stage, middle to old age, in its bearing upon religion. I strongly suspect that not many people really develop the full mental outlook proper to this stage. This is the stage when the adult is biologically freed from the cares of parenthood – his children having become independent adults. His period of parenthood should be a period of preparation for a wider parenthood so he should have developed the psychological attitudes that would prompt him to care for a wider family, the weak and needy beyond his family. Or should he be preparing himself for a new kind of life beyond death? Psychologically it should not be a period of retreat from responsibility.

Since it is in infancy that the foundations of character are laid and the pattern of later mental functioning determined, we need to look more closely at the development that takes place then. We see it under three aspects. First, there is the evolution of the instincts, which seems to follow a constitutionally controlled order. Second, there is the sequence of objects to which the instincts attach themselves to procure the satisfaction they need. Third, there is the developing structure of the mind from the plastic psyche of the new-born infant to the complex Id, Ego, Super-ego system which is achieved by the end of infancy and which is the permanent structure of the developed human mind.

First, then, the evolution of the instincts. There are three main groups: the self-preservative or ego instincts such as food seeking; the sex instincts; and the instinct of aggression. The ego instincts are not as a rule subject to repression at any stage unless they become associated by displacement with the sex instincts and they develop in a straightforward manner adjusting themselves to reality. Hunger is one of the great driving forces of society but it is probably true to say that hunger does not create civilization. Experience tends to show that it disrupts civilization and makes for anti-social behaviour.

The great changes occur in the sex instincts and it is these which supply the energy for most of the creative activities of man, including his religion. The psychoanalytic discoveries about the nature and functioning of the sex instincts form the greater part of Freud's work and it is in this respect that he has done so much to throw light on vast fields of mental and spiritual processes, and it is here also that he has met the greatest criticism, unfortunately all too often misapplied criticism because springing from a failure to understand what he was saying. Psychoanalysis uses the words 'sex' and 'sexual' in a much wider sense than that current in ordinary usage. Since this has led to misunderstandings it has been suggested that some other term should have been found to convey psychoanalytical meanings. Indeed Freud adopted the term 'libido' (adjective 'libidinal') for the energy belonging to the sex instincts. A new term for sex, however, would not have overcome the difficulty, for the real trouble is that the common conceptions of sex are inadequate and the psychoanalysts are right in showing the unity, amid all its strange ramifications and secondary manifestations, of the group of sex instincts. They are not propounding a new philosophic idea but describing facts. Merely changing terms would not bring about the knowledge of how sex functions and its place in the human mind. We do not need a term that is neutral, leaving our ideas unaltered. We need fuller knowledge of the nature of sex. Freud did not set out with his theories of sex developed beforehand. He set out to explore the unconscious mind and he tells us that it was a great surprise to him when he found that, behind all the neuroses he was investigating, there was always a cause which was sexual in nature, and that the unconscious mind is largely made up of repressions of the sex instincts in one form or another and of their derivatives or material that has become attached to them. He was forced to adopt his theory of sex by the material he discovered.

We are apt to think of sex mostly in terms of the adult reproductive form which appears during adolescence and prepares for and presses the individual to the activities of courtship and procreation. We tend to treat earlier manifestations of sex as at most incipient rudimentary forms of this adult instinct. That conception is inadequate. The adult form of sex is not a new development; it is the culmination of a series of stages through which the sex instincts pass, beginning right from birth. The sex life of the infant is not incipient and rudimentary. On the contrary, it is extremely rich and active, and if anything the direct part it plays in infantile life is bigger than in adult life.

In infancy we find not one sex instinct but a number of component instincts, component because they all contribute to the final adult form which takes them up into itself and subordinates their aims to the central aim of intercourse and procreation. These component instincts betray their sexual character by their subsequent entry into the mature sex instinct, which can be traced by the sensual pleasure they afford the infant, and by their clear affinity with adult sexual perversions.

The sexual instincts of the infant develop in a sequence, with one phase overlapping another. We can describe it in another way as sexual excitability focusing itself in a sequence of zones until they reach the mature form of greatest sensitivity in the genital organs. The first phase is auto-erotism, in which the stimulation of various parts of the body gives the infant much pleasure. The mouth rapidly becomes the chief of these zones, no doubt helped by the constant stimulation of sucking and because of the associated satisfactions of taking food. But the development of the phases seems governed by an innate law and does not depend on the accidents of experience, though these may influence quite strongly the degree to which the passage from phase to phase is successfully achieved. Following the first oral or sucking phase is the secondary oral phase, biting. Usually associated with this is a tendency to aggression, shown in the pleasure derived from biting. Sadism, or sensual delight in inflicting pain, generally has its seat in this phase. Next comes the anal-erotic stage where the rectum is the chief source of sexual pleasure and the child shows great interest in the bowel and bladder functions. There are two stages in this phase also. In the first stage the infant gets pleasure from retaining the faeces as long as possible to increase the tension in the rectum. This is a carry over from the sadism of the late oral phase. In the second stage of anal-erotism the pleasure is derived from defecation. If retention of the faeces persists into this stage it is not for its own sake, but is for the sake of the increased pleasure in the greater amount of the defecation. Interest in the excretion of urine tends to supplant that in defecation and the infant then passes into the urethral phase, which may be regarded as the first stage of the phallic phase. The latter is the last stage achieved in infancy. In it the penis becomes the focus of the sexual interest and the zone of greatest excitability. It is the same for both sexes. The little girl imagines that she will grow a penis, if she becomes aware of her lack. The clitoris is looked on as a small penis that will later become larger.

During this period two other pairs of component sexual instincts manifest themselves. We have spoken of sadism, the instinct which is marked by the sensual pleasure gained from inflicting cruelty. Its counterpart is masochism, in which the delight comes from suffering pain or being treated cruelly. The other pair consists of the instinct to exhibit his body that the infant shows, and which lies behind general 'showing off', and its counterpart the instinct of sexual curiosity, the desire to see the bodies and sexual organs of others, which can lead to morbid curiosity.

After the phallic phase is reached and rises to its full height, somewhere about the age of four, in the period of the Oedipus Complex, the sexual instincts pass into a period of latency during childhood and only become active again in puberty, when the biological development of the sex organs initiates another period of sexual growth. The earlier phases of infancy are rapidly and lightly recapitulated and then the instinct passes on into the full genital phase in which intercourse and reproduction become the primary aim and the female gives up the phallic fantasy and accepts her role as child bearer with greatest sensitivity in the vagina rather than the clitoris. The earlier forms of sex are compounded as it were into this final stage and normally give up their independent satisfactions. In so far as they are retained, and they mostly survive in some measure, they lose their independent functioning and serve as preparatory or subsidiary activities heightening the pleasure and power of the main sexual function, as for instance, kissing and courtship serves as an excitation of the genital impulses. If the component impulses survive into adult life as independent satisfactions or are unduly strong in the contribution they make in sexual functioning, we can be confident that there has been some breakdown in the transition from the earliest auto-erotic phase to the final genital phase.

The second line of development, which goes on while the sexual instincts are developing, is the evolution of love objects. A love object is that which the sex instincts seek as a source of gratification and in relation to which they produce the sensual delight which marks their activity, whether it be the pleasure the child gets from running naked before those it loves or whether it be the intense orgasm of the developed instinct. It would be inexact to say that the first love object of the infant is himself, for that implies a consciousness of being a separate individual which the young infant does not at first possess but only acquires gradually. What the infant first loves are the sensations of delight caused by various stimulations, warmth, soft touching of his body, and so on, particularly the sensations derived from sucking. The infant longs for the sensations and so comes to desire the activities and objects, as he learns to recognize them, which cause the sensations. The mother's breast and arms naturally become the chief love object of his early months. They are associated with his most pleasant experience and no doubt are the first objects which he learns to identify. Gradually he associates with them other features of the mother until she begins to emerge in his consciousness as a total person, outside himself, yet the source of his greatest delights, and so something belonging in a most special way to him. He loves her with all his being. That means he experiences his greatest pleasures, all he is capable of, in his various relations with her. To him she is the most beautiful and most desirable thing in the world. He forms an idealised picture of her that tends to remain through later vicissitudes as an unconscious ideal against which all other women are measured. If he does not grow out of this stage in the normal healthy way he will always be seeking the ideal woman and will tend to project the unconscious image of the mother on to someone else whom he will perceive in the preconceived way, unconsciously blinding himself to actual characteristic traits of that person. Or, as we shall see, he may find other mother substitutes, to which he will ascribe the same ideal qualities.

This idealised picture of the mother springs from what she means to him. His love is entirely self-centred. It cannot be anything else. All he knows are the pleasures and pains he suffers, and he seeks to feel pleasure and to get rid of pain and discomfort when it comes to him.

Gradually he learns to distinguish other persons from his mother. The father is probably the next person he separates out as a unity, and then he learns to distinguish persons from things – not in an abstract way, but by learning to recognize the difference in behaviour of individuals and objects which come within his experience. Each of them affords him some opportunities of pleasure, so his love is extended to them. More technical psychoanalytic language would say that his libido (the energy of his sex instincts) attaches itself to them, or he forms libidinal cathexes towards them (a cathexis is the attachment of libido to an object as a source of satisfaction). In the normal life of the infant it is perhaps not misleading to speak of 'love', but some of the displaced attachments of libido diverge so widely from the original activity that it is sometimes an advantage to use the technical term to describe them provided we bear in mind that the original source was a love attachment.

The mother and father are the chief love objects of the infant and they are followed by the other members of the family. Things are loved in a different way but become animated in the fantasies of the infant either as representatives or extensions of himself or else as representatives of other people when the love which could not be satisfied on them, because of their absence or some other reason, has become displaced to the objects now identified in fantasy with them. This is a sign that repression has begun. The infant's libidinal desires are completely egoistic and insatiable for the presence of the loved person, the mother, who is the prototype of all love objects. The mother is unable or unwilling to satisfy all the love demands of the infant. She has other interests, other duties. So the longings of the infant have to be frustrated quite frequently and he experiences the tension of unsatisfied libidinal urges. This is very painful and it tends to turn to anxiety lest he has lost the mother for ever, the source of his love-pleasure. In due course she appears but he has meanwhile known acute pain and he has to deal with that. To avoid the pain he resorts to fantasy – the beginnings of play life – and imagines that the mother is present. One of the toys by him serves as a mother substitute and provides a partial gratification, giving some pleasure and helping to allay the pain and anxiety. This 'as if' process of fantasy becomes a fruitful way of dealing with otherwise unmanageable situations and it provides a bridge to endless transfers of libido to form new attachments. Later on it also becomes a way of working out social relationships. The infant will play out in fantasy the mother's attitude to him by identifying himself with her and treating the toy as his baby. Or he will take the sting out of some situation he fears by acting it out and making it come to the conclusion his libido desires. A rich play life is essential to the development of the child's mind. It enables him to deal with the tensions arising from frustrations, that is, to bring them under control by repression – drawing the consciousness away from the real frustration and providing a substitute satisfaction.

The development of the love objects comes to a crisis in what is known as the Oedipus Complex. We shall have later to examine more fully the significance of the Oedipus Complex and some of its consequences, so we only need here to fit it into the general picture of the stages of development. The Oedipus Complex is the climax of the development, the great finishing drama which helps to complete the structure of the mind. It arises from the love attachment to the mother. The infant's love is completely selfish. He recognizes no other claims on the mother as legitimate and resents whatever comes between him and her. (For the sake of simplicity, we are here considering the case of the boy.) The mother is his special possession and in his mind she loves only him. That is the only way he can think of her. He has not yet acquired objectivity nor any deep sense of the rights of others. It is true that he has had to undergo frustrations which made him think he had lost her and there have been occasions when even in her presence he seems to have lost her love. The loss of the mother's love is the greatest deprivation he knows and the fear of it the greatest source of self-control he has. By the time he is about four years of age he is passing into the phallic stage of sexual development and his attachment to his mother brings him sensual longings in an intense form that drive him to seek to caress her physically and to be caressed by her. He experiences a high degree of almost genital sexual excitement. But he finds his desires frustrated. Instead of sleeping with him, as he imagines she wants to do, she forsakes him and sleeps with the father. The only reason why she does this must be because the father compels her. The father then is his great rival; and an all powerful rival. He wishes him out of the way, wants to destroy him. Since he feels this murder wish towards his father he naturally supposes the father feels the same towards him and so he is afraid of the father. The father wants to destroy his power to love the mother, and that is, he wants to castrate him by cutting off his penis, the centre of his sexual excitation and interests.

Vivid nightmares are characteristic of this period, reflecting the intense emotional strain. In them the boy is pursued by wild animals, such as bulls, or threatened by terrible men or menlike monsters – all representations of the father – as the penalty of indulging in fantasies of possessing the mother. I well remember a dream I had when I was four or five years old. For some reason I cannot remember, I was sleeping with my mother that night. I dreamt that an awful gorilla-like monster came and stood at the head of the bed looking down at me as I lay there helpless, leeringly and leisurely preparing to do violence to me. I woke in terrible fear and to this day the scene of the moonlight streaming through the windows and falling across the bed is one of my clearest memories.

The boy is placed in an unbearable situation. His love makes him desire the mother, but if he gets her he thereby encounters the destructive wrath of the father who will castrate him. He has to choose therefore between his sensual longing for the mother and his fear of castration. The self-love wins and the boy renounces his desires for the mother. He is enabled to do this by a process of great importance. First of all he identifies himself with his father. This he is able to do because he loves him as well as hating him, and because the father does what he himself wants to do – sleeps with the mother. He then introjects the father image into himself, that is, he divides up his mind into two parts, one part being his own self and its desires and the other the identification of himself with his father. He then accepts the commands which (he imagines) the father image gives him and so he is enabled to renounce the sensual desires he feels towards the mother. He represses them and his love towards her loses its sensual quality, becomes 'aim-inhibited' and so transformed into tender affection which does not conflict with the now recognized rights of the father and so does not arouse his wrath.

The foregoing is an over-simplified statement of what occurs in the boy's mind somewhere between the ages of four and seven. We must remember that it is a very complex process with many different phases and strands of development. The mother, for instance, is a rival for the father's love, and there is an inverted Oedipus Complex arising out of this phase, but not so strong because of the greater strength of the hetero-sexual attachment to the mother, who in any case was the chief love object from the earliest months. It is too simple to say that the image introjected is just that of the father. It is a compound of father and mother. Nor has this account made any mention of the many things that may go wrong in this resolving of the Oedipus Complex, such as for instance splitting the mother into two images, one idealised, the other seen as the loose and faithless woman who goes to the father just because she is loose, and who thereby makes sex to the infant an unclean thing. The process outlined here is simply the healthy way of dealing with the Oedipus Complex, and it is part of every normal person's development.

Before we go on to consider the third line of growth, that of the structure of the mind, there are two processes which we should note since they affect the development from stage to stage both of the sex instincts and of the love objects and the inter-connexions between the two lines of development. These are 'fixation' and 'regression'. Fixation occurs when the transition from one stage to the next fails and the mind is arrested or 'fixed' (sometimes called 'fixated') in an early stage of development. For instance there may be fixation in the oral phase of sex or upon the mother as love object. The fixation is rarely if ever absolute. But it means that an unduly strong charge of libido fails to move on freely to the next stage and instead is retained in the earlier form and keeps it active instead of allowing it to become quiescent and be absorbed into the final form. Fixation obviously weakens the later forms of functioning by withdrawing some of the energy that should have belonged to them and by preventing the growth into an undivided unity which should be the normal process. The fixation becomes repressed but being strong it manifests itself through displacement in derived ways of behaviour. The study of character traits due to fixations in the respective phases of development is one of the most interesting parts of psychoanalysis. We cannot elaborate on it here nor can we go into the causes of fixation. It is a subject of supreme importance for education and the care of children as well as for psychotherapy.

Fixation lays the foundation for 'regression'. By weakening the more mature forms of functioning it renders the ego less able to deal with the demands made upon it in these forms in later life. For instance, marriage or the contemplation of it, requires strong development into the genital phase of sex and also the possibility of a psychologically free choice of a partner. The ego, hampered by fixation, feels its inadequacy to cope with the full demands of the situation and under the fear of failure retreats to its strong point, the fixation. If the fixation is in an early sexual phase there may result a failure of true genital functioning and a recrudescence of the characteristic activities of the infantile phase. If it is a fixation on the mother that is the trouble, the man will treat his wife as his mother and the barriers established against sexual activities towards the mother, which were established by introjection of the father image, will operate unconsciously against the wife – who in any case was probably chosen as a mother substitute – and will prevent normal healthy marital relations. This retreat to the fixations is regression. If there is no fixation to establish a weakness in the developed ego there can be no regression.

It only remains now to consider the development in the

structure of the mind as a whole, that is, the genesis of the Id, Ego and Super-ego within the unity of the mind.

The psyche or mind of a new-born infant is totally Id. It has not been modified by contact with reality. In it reside the instincts, hunger, sex, aggression, which, under stimulation from within or without, set free energy that creates tension until it finds expression in appropriate ways through the organs of the body. The perceptive organ of consciousness is attached to the Id, and provides a means by which it can become aware of the real world as well as of its own inner states. The Id is governed entirely by the principle of seeking pleasure and avoiding pain. In general, pleasure comes from the successful discharge of accumulated energy from the instincts and pain from the increase of tension. The infant therefore seeks immediate satisfaction for its needs and cannot bear the pain of waiting. If no other release of tension is available the energy will be dissipated by crying and violent contortions of the body in an outburst of rage that may turn to panic fear.

The mere fact of being alive and conscious brings the infant into contact with reality through his perceptions and builds up a growing store of memories. Some of the instinctive satisfactions come to it from objects in the environment, such as the pleasures of being bathed, and other urges, like hunger, can be satisfied only by the real world. These contacts with reality gradually modify the psyche of the infant and it acquires a store of experiences held in the memory. It learns ways in which to adapt itself to the real world as the most fruitful source of satisfaction. If it is to get these satisfactions it must accommodate itself to the demands of the real world, so on the pleasure-pain system of the primitive Id a second principle of behaviour is imposed, the reality principle. The reality principle directs behaviour according to the observed facts of a situation, to what will work rather than to the impossible immediate pleasure. The infant has to learn to control the desire for immediate satisfaction for the sake of getting a greater but remote one, or sometimes any satisfaction at all. The tension that an instinctive urge builds up is then directed to the most useful steps to gain fulfilment, and not to the rage and panic fear of the pleasure-pain or Id system. The new reality principle, with its store of experiences on which it draws in shaping plans of action, is centred round consciousness. This secondary, reality-adapted system is what we call the Ego. Its primary function is to inhibit the pleasure-pain principle by which the Id works and direct the impulses coming from the Id to effective satisfaction achieved through manipulating the real world. It imposes a check between impulse and action until the possible ways of action are surveyed and a choice made. It establishes itself therefore as the executive organ of the Id.

The Ego has no strength of its own. It draws the energy it needs to control the Id from the Id itself by persuading it in the face of painful frustration to accept the conditions of satisfaction imposed by the real world. The rich fantasy life of the infant acts as a kind of safety valve and reduces the pressure on the Ego. But under the influence of the Oedipus Complex the Id develops a strong demand for total possession of the mother, which the Ego finds difficult to withstand. It cannot offer rich enough substitute satisfactions in place of possessing the mother and finds itself torn in the intolerable conflict between the demands of the Id and the danger of destruction which it fears from the father. It resorts, as we have seen, to the mechanism of introjecting the father (parental) image and turning the fear into an inner means of controlling the Id. The Ego is henceforth divided. It retains in one part of itself the executive function of dealing with the real world. The other part, the modification brought about by introjecting the parental image, becomes a seat of authority sitting above the Ego proper to impose commands upon it which call for obedience. This is the Super-ego, the seat of conscience. By the process of its formation the Super-ego is given unconditional authority over the Ego and it thus supplies the 'ought' of moral standards. It bids the Ego control undesirable impulses and it also represses into the unconscious the impulses it regards as most objectionable and dangerous. Being derived from the Oedipus Complex the Super-ego itself works largely in the unconscious and prevents these impulses reaching consciousness. As well therefore as being the source of judgements of conscience of which we are conscious it is the means of repression. Conscience and repression are therefore very closely allied.

This account of the genesis of the Super-ego shows how it is derived from the sex instincts. The study of the aggressive instincts shows that they make a big contribution to the Super-ego. In the early years the aggressive impulses of the infant threaten to bring it into danger. The feeble Ego can only control them by inverting them, splitting them, as it were, and turning one part to attack and control the rest. This inner aggression forms part of the Super-ego. Where there has been a strong inversion of aggression, therefore, we may expect to find a savage Super-ego in sharp conflict with the Id and constantly criticising the Ego, raising in it feelings of inferiority and of guilt.

We thus see the Ego, the conscious reasoning executive self, in a three-fold bondage. First, it is the servant of the Id and has to direct the Id's impulses or wishes to successful satisfactions in the real world. Secondly, in doing so it has to conform to the standards imposed by the Super-ego and obey its orders. If the Super-ego forbids one line of satisfaction the Ego has to find an alternative line which is acceptable to both Id and Super-ego. Thirdly, the Ego has to master the real world, the only final source of satisfaction. What it can offer to the Id and the Super-ego is therefore limited by the possibilities available in the world. The Ego has to persuade the Id that it is no use crying for the moon, or over spilt milk. Crying may be a safety valve, a leakage of energy as fantasy is, but it achieves nothing. (Unless, of course, the Ego adopts it as a method of working on other people to provide substitute satisfaction.)

In later chapters we shall examine how all this bears on Christianity. It is enough here to note that mental health and strength depends on a just balance between Ego, Id and Super-ego so that the Ego is free to handle the world, yet full of energy for its tasks because in good relations with the

Id, and at the same time under enough control from the Super-ego not to choose the first primitive satisfactions which offer, but to build up its energy for greater, more integrated, and more permanent satisfactions.

Part Two

PSYCHOANALYSIS AND CHRISTIANITY

CHAPTER 6

THE UNCONSCIOUS IN CHRISTIANITY

WE can now pass to a more direct consideration of some of the ways in which psychoanalysis throws light on religious behaviour. We might begin with a general question and ask where religion is centred in the complex structure of the mind. It is not an easy question to answer, if only for the reason that we cannot give a clear definition of religion. Moreover, it would be premature to attempt an answer at this stage since we ought first to see what psychoanalysis contributes to the understanding of the nature of religion. The general topic of this book is to examine whether psychoanalysis gives us any criterion, or at least fresh material, which will enable us to assess more truly whether religion plays a healthy part in human life, and if it does what that criterion is by which we may hope to distinguish the sound from the unsound, the true from the false, in what commonly passes for religion. We are, of course, limiting 'religion' to Christianity except where recourse to illustrations from other religious faiths appears to add something of value.

We have already seen that there is no special religious instinct, but that it is a secondary product of instinctual development. Freud says that the Super-ego is the seat of religion, and there is much truth in his contention. But he bases this assertion on a conception of religion that is not adequate to describe the Christian life and he so blandly ignores the vast amount of scientific, historical study that has been devoted to the sources of Christianity, that his conception is scarcely worth calling even a travesty of it. (See 'A Philosophy of Life', *New Introductory Lectures*, and *The Future of an Illusion*.) We cannot therefore get any direct help from him in answer to our question. Instead of a general answer at this point we shall take up, one by one, various points

73

of interest and see how far they can give us any clue by which to sort the good from the bad in what commonly passes for Christianity. In this chapter we shall deal with the general significance of the unconscious in religion and in succeeding chapters we shall consider the influence of each stage of the child's psychological development upon the forms and attitudes of Christianity.

When we turn to examine a little more closely the part played by the unconscious in Christianity, we are brought up against the question of fantasy and reality in the mind, the two ways of thinking.

As soon as an infant is born he must begin to fend for himself. He must breathe, take food, evacuate. He is subjected also to a wide variety of sensations. Some he finds interesting and pleasure-giving, others provoke dislike, others may be so intense as to be painful. We cannot suppose the new-born infant is able to distinguish himself from the world or indeed that he has any clearly defined perceptions. These only come gradually as the result of considerable experience. The infant's responses must be for the most part involuntary and his world simply a mass of sensations in which no distinction is drawn between memories and reality.

Let us take the case of hunger. The infant grows hungry. He, of course, does not know what is the matter beyond that there is a feeling of discomfort, of uneasiness, of something that he dislikes. If he is not soon fed the discomfort may become so acute as to be painful and its continued presence is likely to provoke fear and create a desire to fly from the pain. The infant reacts by crying and he writhes and squirms in the effort to get away from the unpleasant feeling. And the crying may soon become even panic screaming. Or possibly the presence of the pain may provoke the aggressive instinct to attempt to destroy it, and we perceive the infant in a bad temper. The rage, of course, does not succeed in destroying the hunger and it too may turn into panic if the hunger is not allayed. But something does happen. There follows another series of sensations, the sensations of being held, of sucking and swallowing, of hearing some comforting sounds, of the smell of the mother, especially her breast. At the end of the series the discomfort has gone.

When the cycle has been repeated a number of times the infant will have built up a complex picture of the sequence. A new factor now enters into the sequence. When the need for food begins to grow, it will first produce in the mind images of previous occasions leading to satisfaction. These images do give some measure of satisfaction of the need and temporarily reduce the hunger. But ultimately the sequence leading to real food becomes necessary for final satisfaction. This factor of an imagined satisfaction is a well known one. People who suffer a prolonged starvation diet find their minds, awake or asleep, continually filled with images of food. There is no doubt that it does give some measure of relief to imagine oneself eating vast meals, even though there is no physical satisfaction from it.

The infant is not yet able to discriminate between self and not-self. He lives, as it were, in his sensations. The mother's breast is no more real to him than his image of it or than his feeling of discomfort. He has not yet discovered the difference between image and reality. Hence there is no reason for him to select any one of the sensations as more significant than the others. He may as readily associate the relief he experiences with the crying as with the mother's breast, until the experience is repeated often enough for him to learn the truth. In the sequence he has done four different things. First, he has felt a need, the need for food, even if he doesn't identify it as such. Second, he has wished for the previously experienced satisfaction. Third, he has created an image of that satisfaction by recalling the past. Fourth, he has taken action of different kinds, cried, struggled, and, when the breast appeared, sucked.

There are thus two sources of gratification; the one by imagining the satisfaction, the other by working for it, for we may describe the actions under the fourth heading as work, in so far as they are attempts to change the real world, or at any rate are the forerunners of what will be action aimed at altering the world once the infant learns to distinguish between image and reality. Gratification by imagination we may call wish-fulfilment. Where it is a question of seeking for food the infant must rapidly learn that only the real world gives true satisfaction and dispels need. He goes on creating images of satisfaction when he gets hungry, because that is how the mind works, seeking the easiest way to satisfaction, but he learns to distinguish his imagination from reality.

The case is different with sex instincts. In the early period of the infant's life the sources of sensual pleasure are the sensitive erotogenic zones of the body which the infant is capable of stimulating without outside help. By sucking his own lips, for instance, or by sucking his thumb, he can get the sensual gratification he needs. He is therefore much slower to learn the distinction between imagination and reality than in the case of the food instinct. When he feels the need for the pleasure that comes from sucking his lips, the wish calls up the image of past satisfaction. At the same time, however, he actually sucks his lips and the image and the reality blend into one. It seems to him, therefore, that the wish-fulfilment gives a complete satisfaction. He is not forced to adapt himself to reality to the same extent.

In a later chapter we shall see how he crosses from his own sensations to the world by way of the mother. In this chapter we shall consider some consequences which issue from the dual way of thought that we have just examined in the thinking of an infant. To these two ways of thinking, as we have already seen, Freud gave the names pleasure-pain principle and reality-principle, calling the first the primary system and the other the secondary system, because it develops as a modification of the first.

The Id works according to the pleasure-pain principle and so, of course, does the unconscious, which is that part of the Id which is subjected to repression. The Ego works by the reality-principle. It has, as we say, a 'reason' for every action, whereas the Id, including the unconscious, wishes to have this or that or do this or that just to get pleasure from it and does not feel any need to justify its wishes. The Id has no direct contact with reality so it draws no distinction between fantasies or imagined satisfaction and real objects. To the Id a fantasy is as real as fact. This is most important to remember when we come to consider the meaning of the feeling of guilt and its sources.

We have already seen how the unconscious finds displaced expression when its direct wishes are repressed. The displaced expression readily assimilates itself to action or belief that is otherwise justified on rational reality-principle grounds and adds its reinforcement to it from the unconscious. Since the Ego is debarred from recognizing a displacement as such, it regards the supposed reasons for the action as wholly adequate to explain it. The only way a displacement can be detected is by uncovering the repression behind it and thereby neutralising the contribution of the unconscious to the form and vigour of the action or belief. One sign that a hidden displacement is present (though it does not reveal the nature of the displacement) is given by the behaviour of someone whose action and the reason for it are subjected to searching questioning or criticism. The resistance or repressing factor begins to work and the person either grows angry or feels a sense of anxiety. This is because the displacement is subjective in its nature, whereas true reasons are objective. If, therefore, criticism of the reasons for our actions and beliefs provokes us to heat (which, by the way, the onlooker observes more readily than we) we can be sure that the unconscious has played a large part in producing them.

The extent to which our conduct is influenced by the unconscious depends of course on the severity of the repressions in each person. But the stages of development are constitutionally determined and fixations in all of them of greater or less severity occur in most people and are repressed to form complexes, or unconscious tendencies, so we find that there are regularly recurring unconscious themes in all fields of human thought, including religion, that get their expression under cover of other ideas.

The unconscious is mainly formed in the period of infancy. After the resolution of the Oedipus Complex any material added to the unconscious gets drawn there because it is closely associated in some way with material already repressed. The unconscious is the infantile mind retaining the wishes, fantasies and judgements of the infantile mind. That is why we remember so little of our experiences of infancy, and why most of the memories we do have are probably false, or considerably distorted, judging by the evidence from many analyses of such memories. It is formed of repressions of the sex and aggressive instincts. The ego-instincts, typified by the food seeking impulse, are on the whole adapted readily to reality and so not subject to repression. Hence behind much of our conduct, colouring our beliefs and shaping our judgements, lie fantasies derived from the repressed sex and aggressive instincts in their various stages of development. They are controlled by the pleasure-pain principle and their aim is wish-fulfilment. They produce wishful thinking.

Wishful thinking is a term frequently misapplied. It does not mean the free indulgence in wishing – 'If wishes were horses, beggars would ride.' It means thinking dominated by the unconscious, that is, directed by unconscious wishes or by wishes that are not necessarily unconscious but whose connexion with the thinking is unconscious. It describes readiness to believe statements or arguments which are in accord with our wishes and to disbelieve or ignore what is opposed to them. Optimism is sometimes a form of wishful thinking – belief that everything will turn out all right because we want it to do so. It is different from confidence based on a fair appraisal of the facts. Thus there is a great difference between believing in God because we want everything to turn out well and having faith that everything will turn out well because we have sound reasons for believing in God. But it is not easy for us to sort out our real motives.

Psychoanalysis seems to indicate that the ideal of mental health is for the Ego, or seat of conscious intelligence, to be as free as possible from bondage to the unconscious and the fantasies which it activates. Its justification for this is three-fold. In the first place, if the Ego is greatly weakened by an overstrong unconscious, the result is a mental illness which no one would regard as desirable. Secondly, we cannot escape the fact that human beings are part of the real world and human life is largely if not wholly made up of relations with other real persons and things and it is therefore desirable that we should have the fullest and most accurate knowledge possible of the real world in which we live, and that is only possible if the influence of the unconscious is reduced to a minimum. Thirdly, the impulses and desires prompted by the instincts find their most enduring and thorough satisfaction through the working of the reality-principle. A patient once said after a relatively light analysis which cured him of some neurotic symptoms, 'I think I am now living at about eighty per cent of my efficiency. If that is a correct estimate, I was only living at about thirty per cent before I was analysed.' In other words the personality is more itself when the Ego is free.

On the other side we note that some of the achievements of thought or action reckoned great in history have been the work of men whose lives have been dominated by some powerful unconscious complex. One illustration will suffice. Dr Ernest Jones, perhaps the leading Freudian in Britain, has very convincingly argued that Shakespeare wrote *Hamlet* under the stresses of his own Oedipus Complex, taking a plot that is one of the standard variations of the Complex and embodying in the character of Hamlet the conflicts, repressions and fantasies which belong to it. Not that Shakespeare meant to do this. His artistic insight and power of selecting essentials enabled him to present a character as real and as consistent as any revealed in an analyst's case book – with the added quality of supreme literary worth. We may conclude, then, that the greatest play in history would have been lost if Shakespeare had not had this unconscious drive to give shape to his play. Against this it might be maintained that the play is only great because it is dealing with an unconscious conflict that is universal. If we were all ideally developed mentally the play would have less meaning and interest for us. However that may be, it is true that unconscious complexes can drive men to concentrate their lives in one direction and if they couple great ability with the fixed drive they may achieve great things. Therefore, in such cases, while it may not be best for the individual's peace of

The other sense in which Christianity is an other-worldly or supernatural religion is that it maintains that this world, and especially human life, is not self-explanatory but requires another to give it meaning. This is a confused and difficult conception. There can be no direct evidence of such a world, for any evidence brought forward would naturally derive its nature from this world. At most the existence of another world transcending and explaining this one must be an inference from failure of naturalistic principles to account for the totality of natural phenomena. Or perhaps the very nature of the modes of thought drives us beyond this world in the search for an explanation of it. Again that is attainable only by a very few people, and the various explanations that these philosophers achieve are seldom completely convincing to more than themselves. In other words, philosophers may attempt to justify belief in another world; their work is not the primary reason for the belief being held.

Christianity has also inherited this belief from other religions. It is linked up closely with belief in survival after death but does not depend on it. Its core is belief in the existence of God, and the study of comparative religion shows that belief in God is a refinement of primitive animism through reason working on experience. It is clear that, once we accept the hypothesis of an order of existence other than this one, monotheism is far more reasonable than animism, polytheism, or any other of its antecedents. But we must ask why we should accept the hypothesis of an other-world. Since there is no direct evidence to support it and only a few philosophically minded people are capable of weighing the abstract arguments in support of the belief, and they differ over the validity of the reasons advanced, again we must assume that belief in God, carrying with it belief in an other-world, was first accepted as a wish fulfilment. The real source of the belief was the unconscious projection of an image in the mind. We have not had much occasion hitherto to refer to this psychological mechanism. By means of it the Ego transfers on to the external world something from the unconscious. In a later chapter we shall see in more detail how it works to produce the idea of God.

Here we are simply concerned to note the fact that this idea did not begin as something directly observed in the world, but, like the idea of survival, is a product of the unconscious. Again we must note that this does not necessarily mean that the idea is false. There are, I believe, valid reasons to justify the other-worldly character of Christianity, but there is no escaping the possibility, some would say probability, that we believe in it because we wish it to be true and the 'proofs' are developed after the belief as rationalizations.

The use of symbols in Christianity reveals a relationship to the unconscious different from that we have just seen in considering the other-worldly character of its beliefs. We take symbolism in its widest meaning to include symbolic acts and symbolic modes of thought as well as symbolic signs and objects. Christianity is not alone in its use of symbols. Symbolism is a constant feature of the mind and it is the chief method of thought used by the Id and the unconscious. The symbol has an economic value in terms of energy because it can gather into itself an infinite variety of associations which in themselves may be contradictory. We may remind ourselves that the early Church called the Creed the symbol of the Faith.

There is a rich field to be explored in tracing out the unconscious associations which generally attach themselves to the various symbols of Christianity – the cross, baptism, communion, the ceremonies of public worship, and so on. The point I want to make is this: symbolism in Christianity is effective in drawing to itself a great many of the unconscious forces of the mind. This is partly shown by the enormous attraction that religion has for the neurotic. Anyone who has to do with a church knows how strong that attraction is.

Christianity has adopted symbolism partly because of the convenience of symbols in expressing ideas compactly, partly because the symbols themselves proved in practice so effective over the human mind, because they bind together many diverse strands of the mind. The symbols capture repressed tendencies because the unconscious seizes upon the symbols to get displaced outlet for repressions. Religion thus draws the forbidden impulses to strengthen belief or action which consciously was intended to have a different character. Some would call this sublimation, but we have seen reason to question this easy use of the word.

Meditative prayer is an effective method of capturing the unconscious. It is like fishing in the deeps of the mind with symbols for bait. The difference is that though the fish are caught readily enough the fisherman (the conscious) never sees the fish. Of course, this is not the only effect of prayer. It is, however, a common result of some types of prayer and it is important in the total picture. For we may well ask whether we don't get a repetition of the story told in the limerick about the young lady of Riga. Deliberately or not, Christianity sets out to capture the unconscious. In the measure that it does so it is able to produce a religion of greater emotional fervour and perhaps more vigorous action. But there is a constant danger of the unconscious wishes taking charge once they have been admitted. They enter in disguise and the unconscious is extremely adept in taking command of a situation. This is a very real danger and in succeeding chapters we shall see that there is very good ground for supposing that the unconscious plays too large a part in shaping the ideas and aspirations of much that is called Christianity. To safeguard against this danger in prayer we need to set understanding on an equal level with devotion. It is not enough to aim at piety, to be as harmless as doves. We need also to be as wise as serpents. Prayer is essential to Christian life and it has its healthy forms. We cannot analyse them here because at this point we are engaged in examining the way the unconscious may influence and even control otherwise healthy activities of the mind, not in making a complete analysis of Christianity.

One final point before we end this section. Psychoanalysts note that under conditions of hardship, when privations are forced upon the individual's instinctive desires because the real world does not yield them satisfaction, the mind regresses from reality to fantasy. The common example of this is day-dreaming, but that is only the most superficial sign. Now Christianity in some respects is a religion of hardship. It offers hope to the poor, the sick, the prisoner, the oppressed, here or in the world to come. It is sometimes at its greatest strength when conditions are hardest, as seems to have been the case in occupied Europe during the second world war. It is essential to Christianity to take thought for the downtrodden, but this creates the danger that it may appeal to them as an exalted daydream and turn their minds permanently to fantasy and away from reality. It was because he believed this is the actual effect of Christianity that Marx called religion the opiate of the people. 'Comfort in adversity' may mean strengthening if we take the old meaning of 'comfort'. The word, however, has degenerated to mean sentimental solace. So may our conception of the Christian Gospel of good news. When it becomes the hope of compensation for hardship and suffering the question for us is whether that is really Christianity.

To sum up, then. In this chapter we have been considering some of the ways in which the unconscious, with its pleasure-pain aims, its fantasies and its wishful thinking, may influence our religious beliefs and conduct without our being aware of it. The value of psychoanalysis is that it reveals this danger to us and enables us to lay more emphasis on the positive reality-principle factors which support Christianity, assuming, that is, that religion is more properly a function of the Ego than of the Unconscious and the Id. The part played by the Super-ego will be considered later.

CHAPTER 7

LIFE AND DEATH

LET us now turn to the influence of particular phases of development upon our fundamental Christian beliefs. The proper place to start is no doubt with the experience of birth.

The Bible begins the story of man with the tale of the Garden of Eden and his expulsion from it. It does so with a sure intuition, for that is the beginning of everyone's life. In the womb the unborn child has an idyllic existence. He knows no hunger, no cold, no shock, for he is fed and warmed and protected from disturbance. He is not required to make the slightest effort except the slow preparation to be born. He cannot have any clear consciousness, for consciousness depends on disturbance, on change, on nervous tension, on perception, and these must be practically unknown in the womb. Then comes birth. The infant is thrust violently out of his haven, never more to return, and in the process is subjected to severe pressure. If he doesn't know pain then, he experiences it with the first breath he draws. And that first breath is also the beginning of effort. He has entered a hard world where struggle is the normal thing, struggle and tension and pain. And it is not only a painful world as the infant meets it. It is a glaring, noisy, cold, rough world in sharp contrast to the world from which he has just come. It is full of strange sensations. He cannot identify them of course, but they all clamour to him for attention and he wants to escape, to get back to the dreamy effortless life of the womb which probably he has only been made aware of by the contrast of the new world he has entered. Then firm hands bathe him and wrap him up warmly in soft clothes and set him down in a snug place. The worst of his new sensations disappear and he falls asleep and thereby recovers for a while the state of Elysium which he had had in the womb.

It is not the same and it is only temporary. The source of nourishment which hitherto sustained his life has been cut off by birth and soon a new sensation, that of hunger, begins to disturb him. First it comes as a gentle uneasiness, then tension mounts to uncomfortableness and finally it becomes a pain from which the baby wants to be free. The need comes upon him like an enemy attacking from without. He struggles to escape the pain, the danger which threatens him and which has driven him again from recaptured Elysium. His effort to escape can only take the form of struggling and crying. He is persuaded to take nourishment by his mouth, which means further effort and new sensations. The pain ceases, the inner tension relaxes and sleep comes to restore the state of bliss once more.

The baby is now launched upon the recurring cycle of life. The cycle begins when an internal or external stimulus creates a need; then tension rises to discomfort and pain; effort follows to deal with the tension; this leads to satisfaction if the effort is successful; and the cycle ends with the bliss of relief from all disturbance. New needs develop as his experience of the world accumulates and his growing instincts flow over into new forms of expression. The cycles of need and satisfaction grow more and more complex and inter-connected. To the simple bodily needs soon are added the social needs of being petted and talked to by his mother; his interest in and need of the world around him grows, with its attractions of light, colour, sound, feel, movement. In a couple of years his desires of mind and body become infinite in number and complexity. They begin to conflict with each other. Some get repressed and function in the unconscious, finding indirect and some-times extremely distorted forms of satisfaction. Some needs are simple and can be fulfilled in a second, others so complex that they take a lifetime for fulfilment and integrate into them-selves an infinity of smaller cycles. But conscious or un-conscious, simple or complex, the pattern remains funda-mentally the same and the cycle goes on until death comes to put an end to need and pain and striving in this world.

There are two tendencies corresponding to the phases of each cycle. There is on the one hand the tendency which drives towards action. The felt need, the search for satisfaction, leads him to make use of his experience of the world so as to control himself and master his environment by overcoming obstacles. On the other hand, there is the tendency to seek for quiescence, for a state of complete non-disturbance. The first is the rising state of tension – the second is its dissipation. Man is a kind of battlefield in which these two tendencies fight out the battle; or rather, man is the battle itself. The texture of his life is woven out of the conflict of the two.

So far as mind is concerned the prototype of quiescence is the womb life. For the body ultimately it is the state of in-organic matter in which there is no life at all. Perhaps we should look beyond that, since nuclear fission has given us an example of the forces pent up in matter, and look to the state of complete quiescence as that state of the universe towards which physicists tell us the material universe is moving, in which all forms of energy will have been finally changed to heat dissipated at random throughout a vast empty space – in effect nothingness. Seen from the psychologist's view point, however, we can put the final victory of the tendency making for quiescence at the point where death puts an end to life.

For these two tendencies Freud adopts the terms 'life instinct' and 'death instinct'. His discussion of them in his book, *Beyond the Pleasure Principle*, is in some ways the most difficult piece of his work to understand. Part of the confusion arises from the use of the word 'instinct' in this connexion. The 'life instinct' and the 'death instinct' are not further instincts to be grouped alongside the ego, sex and aggressive instincts. Rather they are ways in which these instincts func-tion in co-operation or in conflict. Thus aggression, with its urge to kill, to destroy, embodies the death instinct admirably. It breaks down the creative construction of the life instinct. And since an unconscious inner impulse has usually been projected on to the object against which the aggression is aimed, the death instinct working in the aggression is in reality attacking the self in the form of the projected impulse rather than the external object, since it is that which makes the object appear dangerous. Sometimes the death instinct can serve the purpose of the life instinct. Thus sleep, which is the temporary victory of the death instinct, serves as a refreshment and re-creation of the life instinct. The point that Freud makes is that these are two active tendencies in the mind and that the terms are not merely descriptive names for groups of mental processes. It is confusing to use 'instinct' in two ways but his terminology has been generally accepted by psychoanalysts so we may adopt it too, remembering this distinction between the life and death instincts and the other instincts.

The death instinct gains the final victory in death, final so far as this world is concerned, and for the moment we must limit our consideration to it, though the attitude of Jesus is relevant to the question of a continuation of life beyond earthly death. The victory of the death instinct does not come because it looks forward. It looks back, back to the state from which the life instinct thrust the individual, back to the state of quiescence which is typified in the effortless life of the womb. Death means to the unconscious a return to the womb. This is illustrated by the custom widespread among primitive peoples of burying the dead in the foetal position, perhaps also by the more modern custom of enclosing the corpse in a coffin. Psychoanalysts know that the coffin is an unconscious symbol of the womb. And in any case the earth is a mother symbol – is it not called Mother Earth? – and to be returned to her is to re-enter the womb.

The longing to return to the womb is one of the strongest entrenchments of the death instinct. Birth is probably the pro-foundest experience that anyone can undergo and it leaves an enduring mark on everyone. With some people it becomes almost a crippling experience which permanently enfeebles them for living or leaves an inner weakness which is always liable to manifest itself should such individuals in later life come under severe strains, either from frustration or deprivation or because circumstances demand unusual effort from them. This may be because they are constitutionally weak in the life instinct or it may be because of an exceptionally severe birth or because of bad treatment soon after birth. The longing to return to the womb then becomes of abnormal strength and hampers the Ego in its efforts to face up to the demands of life.

The womb fantasy is repressed into the unconscious and from there it finds various ways of expressing itself and influencing the aims and beliefs of the person concerned. Like every other repression it can produce neurotic symptoms. A patient undergoing analysis had a habit of closing his eyes and imagining that he was crawling through a dark narrow tunnel. He felt tightly constricted and suffered such an agony of fear that he would sweat profusely, but he could not refrain from torturing himself by this fantasy. He was living over again in a symbolic form not far removed from the actual the experience of his birth. The death instinct was strong in him and he was trying to reverse the process of birth and re-enter the womb.

Such neurotic manifestations of the womb fantasy are common. One element in them is the fear of being born, the fear of a new world, of facing up to new situations, with new demands on one's energy and love. It is the common desire to preserve the old and familiar, the *status quo*. These fears – fear of change, of new demands, of having to meet new people – and others like them are quite common in people whom we should hesitate to class as neurotic. It is never easy to draw the line between the normal and the abnormal. The chief characteristic of neurotic behaviour is that it exaggerates some feature of mental life out of all proportion to the part it plays in the normal, or else that it manifests it out of its proper stage of development. An adult who persistently talks baby fashion is a nauseating phenomenon whom we should class as definitely neurotic (I am not speaking of those cases of retardation of mental development for glandular or other physiological reasons), but should we not also classify as neurotic those people who retain their infantile attitude to their parents in their behaviour to their parent substitutes, such as God?

The tendency of the death instinct is to halt development. Nevertheless it has its part in the normal healthy life. The clearest normal manifestation of the death instinct and the desire to return to the womb is in sleep. In sleep the mind withdraws the attachment of its energy from the world, it gives up, to use more technical language, its cathexes on objects. This is a reversal of the birth process by which the mind is led to reach out after the objective world and establish points of contact and interest with it whereby it gets expression for its instinctive impulses and the satisfaction of its needs. Sleep means cutting oneself off from the world, a return of the energy back into the self. At the same time it enables us to restore and add to the energy which has been consumed in the waking period before sleep. Periodic sleep is a necessary and proper part of the normal rhythm of life. Less proper, however, is the constant weariness or lethargy which afflicts some people, who find all life a burden and constantly long for death as a release. In less extreme forms we find them yearning for a 'quiet' life (as distinct from an ordered one), or wishing they were 'cows in a field' with no worries to bother them. The death instinct lies heavy on such people. They are scarcely normal. It seems likely that the normal should comprise periods of tiredness and refreshment alternating.

As with so many of the wishes we have buried in our unconscious in growing up, the womb fantasy has been enshrined in the mythology and fairy stories of the world. Almost universally people have looked back to a golden age of idyllic happiness, an age of innocence and virtue – though here another strand of fantasy has joined itself to the first. Or they have believed in some 'Islands of the Blessed'. The womb fantasy has not confined itself to myth and fairy story. It has crept into every day thinking, into philosophy and into political science. We often look back on childhood as the period of greatest happiness, contrary to all evidence, reading into our early days the unconscious bliss of the womb life. Children, we think, have no cares, no responsibilities, no anxieties. Yet actual observation shows childhood torn with anxieties and conflicts. It is in childhood that we suffer our worst nightmares, symptoms of frustration, fear and inner conflict. And the older generation nearly always looks on the present one as going from bad to worse. Things were always better when we were young; manners and morals were finer. The olden days were golden days. The philosophic cult of the 'noble savage', grand in his uncorrupted simplicity, a belief that is contrary to all that history and anthropology can teach

91

us, is another instance of the same backward-looking tendency. If we are driven by study of the facts to recognize that the golden age never existed in the past we put it into the future. It will come, magically, somehow. Like the glorification of the past, our dream cities, our utopias, our hope of a Promised Land, are the expression of an overstrong death instinct driving us to flee from the frustrations and pains and struggles of life to the magical ease of the womb. So was the optimism of the nineteenth century with its belief that science had ushered in an era of unending moral and material progress. Karl Marx was in most ways a realistic thinker, aware of the conflicts of the world. Perhaps it was because conflict so engrossed him that he created a new myth embodying the womb fantasy. The communist utopia, the stateless community in which all men will work for the good of everyone, is going to come into being with effortless ease once the dictatorship of the proletariat has finally abolished capitalism. It is no less a fantasy of womb life than is the dream of riches of the poor man who believes that with riches his cares would disappear, he could stop work and 'enjoy life', when all the evidence denies that riches are a source of happiness and virtue.

The classic poetic expression of the womb fantasy was given by Wordsworth in his *Intimations of Immortality*:

> Our birth is but a sleep and a forgetting:
> The soul that rises with us, our life's star,
>   Hath had elsewhere its setting,
>   And cometh from afar:
>   Not in entire forgetfulness,
>   And not in utter nakedness,
> But trailing clouds of glory do we come
>   From God who is our home:
> Heaven lies about us in our infancy!
> Shades of the prison house begin to close
>   Upon the growing boy,
>   But he beholds the light, and whence it flows
>   He sees it in his joy:
> The youth, who daily farther from the east
>   Must travel, still is Nature's Priest,

And by the vision splendid
Is on his way attended;
At length the Man perceives it die away,
And fade into the light of common day.

Wordsworth is not here writing about the Christian hope of immortality, but about a haunting memory of a life more real, more glorious than that of 'the common day', in fact, about the womb life.

The story of the Garden of Eden is the greatest of the birth myths. It is unique in that it gets its emphasis right and the magnificence of its truth deserves to be emphasized in view of the fact that too many people read it as an ordinary womb fantasy – something desirable lost. Adam and Eve were set in the garden of delight where life was easy and they had all they needed and they were innocent. Their nakedness is another sign that this refers to the womb life. They were driven forth from the Garden (birth) and Adam is condemned to a life of toil (reality-principle). He must win his bread by the sweat of his brow. Effort replaces ease. But here is the point: God sets an angel with a flaming sword at the entrance to the Garden to see they do not get back. There is no turning back in the life which God appoints. We are ordained by God to live a life of toil and struggle. That is the norm, the ideal. The Garden of Eden existence is not the ideal, it is the fantasy, the illusion of life. The story as told in the Book of Genesis adds another significant point though it inverts the order and so partially goes astray. In the Bible story Adam and Eve were cast out of the Garden because they ate of the fruit of the tree of the knowledge of good and evil. The truth is that the knowledge of good and evil is the result, not the cause, of being born. So too with the clothing of themselves.

There are other elements in the story, such as the sense of guilt, which express unconscious wishes springing from other sources than the womb fantasy. They will be dealt with in chapter 11. It is the almost invariable rule that a number of strands from different levels of the unconscious unite to create the one symptom or fantasy; and it is the case with the Garden of Eden story. In addition, the elements of the story have been worked over by the conscious mind to give logical sequence and this accounts for the inversions we find in it. But even as it stands it is one of the greatest stories ever told.

This theme of life and death – the conflict of the life and death instincts – constantly recurs in the Bible. 'Behold, I have set before you life and death, choose life.' 'I came that they may have life, and may have it abundantly.' These are typical. Jesus insisted on the primacy of the life instinct. His mission was to overcome death in all its forms. He does not leave us in doubt as to what he thought life involves. 'Whosoever would save his life shall lose it.' 'Narrow is the gate, and straitened the way, that leadeth into life, and few be they that find it.' 'No man, having put his hand to the plough, and looking back, is fit for the kingdom of God.' It is almost in the direct language of Freud that he says: 'Follow me. Leave the dead to bury their own dead.' He does not preach asceticism as an end in itself. But he recognizes the law of life that he who would go forward to life must face and accept hardship and struggle and loneliness and suffering. The easy way is the way of death, not because it is easy, but because it is a turning back from effort and struggle. 'Wide is the gate, and broad is the way that leadeth to destruction, and many be they that enter in thereby.'

The choice of struggle is not for the sake of asceticism, but for the richer satisfactions that it brings. 'In him was life and the life was the light of men,' said St John. 'Who for the joy that was set before him endured the cross, despising the shame', said St Paul. It is significant that Jesus described the entry into the new life as a rebirth. 'Ye must be born again.' That is the keynote of the eternal life he offers. It is not something magical, some mysterious process; it is a simple statement of the way in which the life instinct overcomes the death instinct. The rhythm of life remains constant; tension, rising perhaps to pain, effort, satisfaction, rest, tension again, and so on, with progress to richer satisfactions. Each cycle is like being born again, for it drives us to face the world where alone we can fulfil ourselves, but the condition of going forward is not to look back, not to desire the process, the flow of life, to cease. If we choose the struggle and its satisfactions, the death that follows each achievement of satisfaction becomes a preparation, a stepping-stone to the next cycle, just as sleep is both the end of one day's work and the gathering of fresh energies for the next. In that way the death instinct is made to serve the life instinct. Death is neither a final haven nor a necessary enemy, it can be made a servant of life. It was because he believed in life that Jesus could face death calmly. The story which begins in the Garden of Eden, with birth to a new life, ends on Calvary Hill, where Christ accepts death as an instrument of life, another birth as it were, and the Resurrection is the demonstration that he was right. To save one's life, one must be prepared to lose it. It is only when we yield to death and try to save what we have, to stay where we are, that death ceases to be the servant of life and succeeds in destroying it.

This analysis of the parts played by the life and death instincts, the drive of the death instinct for a return to the womb, and Christ's inexorable choice of the life instinct, throws light upon the Christian conceptions of life in this world and the next. It affects, for instance, our conceptions of what it means to accept Christianity and receive the grace of God. We should not look for life to be made easy for us. Some people are disheartened when in genuine sincerity they have made some active profession of faith, been converted or confirmed, and find that they still have to struggle against temptations to do evil. Such people have a mistaken idea of what true Christianity offers. It offers the grace and power that come from communion with God to reach heights of living, of self-realization, and so of happiness, that are impossible without them. But the heights cannot be reached without struggle. To suppose that conversion will make us good in the sense that we shall not have to struggle against sin any more is to indulge in a form of the womb fantasy, for it is to look for a spiritual life of security and bliss that comes without our putting forth effort. The Christian cannot hope to find life easier than Christ found it and the Gospels bear witness to the fact that all that he did cost him great effort.

It throws light too on what ought to be our attitude in

prayer. Too often prayer is a petition to God to make things easy for us, if not materially at least morally, by removing from us the need to struggle, by exercising some kind of magic upon us. Our attitude is that we can leave it all to God, that we have done all we need to do when we have 'cast our care on God'. We should not pray for protection, but for courage and achievement that we may be effective instruments to do the will of God.

Perhaps the womb fantasy is not so likely to distort our thinking about religion in this world as it is our conceptions of Heaven. Paradoxical as it may seem, it is about Heaven, almost the same word as haven, that the death instinct has freest rein and the womb fantasy through which it so often works given free play. No doubt this is because Heaven *is* closely associated with the idea of death.

It is interesting to compare the conceptions of the after-life which belong, at least in their popular form, to the four great religions, Hinduism, Buddhism, Mohammedanism and Christianity, and see how much they have in common. Hinduism teaches that the ultimate attainment of the soul is re-absorption into Brahma, the source of all things. Maia, the veil of illusion which is the cause of the feeling of individuality, will be dissolved away and only the eternal unity of all things will remain. Life with its sufferings and struggles is unreal. Man's destiny is to return to that from which he came, or rather, to lose the illusion of having come from it. In other words, birth is not real, life is not real. Death prevails. Buddhism looks for Nirvana, extinction of the individual, a plain longing for death. The goal of Nirvana is reached by giving up all desire, that is, by retreating completely from the life instinct, for the essence of life is desire. But though Buddhism seems to describe Nirvana in negative terms, as nothingness, it is somehow a state of bliss, positive nothingness. It is hard to imagine a conception more suited to describe life in the womb, which can only be known by the contrast which is brought about by being born. Buddhism, then, clearly sets up the fantasy of return to the womb as the highest goal of man. Mohammedanism, like Christianity, does not look forward to the extinction of individual existence, so the victory of the death instinct is not so complete in it as in Hinduism and Buddhism. But the life which it holds out in prospect for the faithful, at least for the men, is one of indulgence and ease, of the removal of the limitations which earthly existence is apt to impose. The death instinct holds sway here because it is the renunciation of effort and struggle, and is a longing, as it were, for the flesh-pots of Egypt. Is Christianity any better? There is no very clear conception of Paradise and Heaven in Christianity but on the whole it does not indulge in such sensual dreams as does Mohammedanism. The sensuality is mental, not physical, in nature. The dominant ideal seems to be to 'gaze and gaze' on God. The colourful imagery of the Book of Revelation need not be taken too literally, but most Christians look to Heaven as a place where pain and sorrow will be done away (with or without a preliminary purification in Purgatory), a place where there will be no more tears, no more struggle. It will be a life of blissful repose. From Christian hymns we gather that this state goes on for ever and ever, broken only by a few hymns of adoration of God, and 'casting down of golden crowns'. The womb fantasy is here allowed to take control, and such a conception of Heaven is a clear victory of the death instinct.

None of these conceptions, Hindu, Buddhist, Mohammedan or Christian, in these popular forms at least, can be correct if they are intended to represent life. The so-called Christian Heaven is in complete opposition to Christ's teaching about the nature of life. When he taught about life he drew no distinction between the character of life on earth or in Heaven. It is all part of the life eternal, and, as we have seen, he was fully conscious of the pull of the death instinct seeking to drag life downwards and the forward surge of the life instinct to create new activities, new satisfactions, mastering the death instinct to its own creative purposes. He insisted on the life instinct as expressing the true nature of God and man. 'My father worketh and I work' aptly sums up his conception of the activity of God and of man. 'I must work the works of Him who sent me.' Man's destiny is to share in the creative action of God. That is the true quality of Christian life.

We need, then, a new theology of Heaven, one that will do justice to the life instinct. It is not for us here to undertake it but we can at least point out that it must involve the cycle of tension, effort, satisfaction, tension, in the terms of the nature of the life after death. That surely means that in Heaven too there must be frustration, striving and pain, for these are the conditions by which the life instinct is able to develop to new and higher things. One might almost say, out of agony (in its proper sense of striving to the utmost) God made the heavens and the earth. Certainly the agony in the Garden and the pain on the Cross were not the signs of death. They were the birth pangs of a fuller life, Christ's Resurrection life.

CHAPTER 8

THE BRIDGE TO THE WORLD

ONCE he is born, every infant is faced with the task of getting outside himself into the real world from which his own individuality divides him. It is a momentous step. The most incurable forms of madness are those which involve a repudiation of reality, like schizophrenia and paranoia. The more tenuous our grip of reality the more prone we are to illusions and the less able to enter into healthy relations with our fellow men. We become disruptive elements in society. Failure to cross from self to reality is the greatest of sins. We shall in this chapter examine more closely how this is achieved.

The bridge by which we cross is the mother. We have seen how in the new-born child instincts are active from the very beginning and we have seen also that the ego instincts, typified by food seeking, tend to lead him to the real world for satisfaction. The richest of the instincts are the sex instincts. They provide the energy for all the cultural life of men and it is through them that the life instinct chiefly, if not entirely, works. It is on what happens to them that mental health (and mental must be understood in the widest sense) chiefly depends. We have glanced very briefly at their normal evolution in the individual, but they are so complex and the ways so infinite in which they can be shaped, either directly or in reaction, by circumstances that it is probably true to say that the perfect development seldom if ever occurs. Instead, we are all subject in some measure to abnormal developments, that is, departures from the norm or pattern of the perfect standard. Fixations are among such abnormalities.

These abnormalities tend to occur at the various stages or crises of mental growth. One of the most important of these happens in the first year, probably the first few months, of life. The young baby sucking his mother's breast gets the satisfaction of his hunger instinct and at the same time the sensual pleasure which comes from the stimulation of his lips and tongue, one of his sensitive 'erotogenic zones' (areas of the body which provide the satisfactions of the sex instincts, especially in their infantile forms. See above, chapter 5). He gets 'libidinal' satisfaction from the sucking and may develop the habit of making sucking movements when not taking food, simply for the pleasing sensation. At this stage the infant is not conscious of himself as an entity nor of a world of objects. He lives in and through his sensations. In due course and little by little, he comes to recognize a world outside himself – to divide the sensations he experiences into two aspects, the sensation itself, with its quality of intimacy, and the cause of it. The first object differentiated out in this way is almost certainly the mother's breast, as we have seen. Gradually he adds to this first object until he has learned to know himself as set in a whole world of objects. The borderline between self and the world is never clearly drawn. Apart from any philo-sophical questions about the relations of mind and matter, psychologists have shown that in the very processes of per-ceiving the world of objects the mind makes its own con-tribution through the process called apperception, so that it is extremely difficult at times to say what is subjective and what is objective. The further light thrown by psychoanalysis on the way the unconscious can determine what we perceive and how we perceive it must increase the doubt we feel about the ordin-ary assumption that we can readily distinguish what is our-selves and what is the 'real' world. Nevertheless, while there always may be aberrations and while it is not easy to delimit the knower from the world he knows, it is yet indisputable that he does come to distinguish between self and the world.

When the primary undifferentiated sensation of breast-sucking-pleasure comes to be divided into recognition of the breast and the pleasurable sensations of sucking it, it is of the greatest significance for the future of the child to which side of the division the libido attaches itself. It may go to the mother's breast, which then becomes a love object, or it may go to the subjective sensations, the nucleus of the later developed self. These, of course, are the extremes and between them lie gradations, but we need to examine the extremes. If the libido goes to the mother, the object choice is called 'anaclitic' (leaning-up-against) because it follows the hunger instinct which has to seek objective satisfaction. If the libido attaches itself to the subjective sensations and the fantasies about pleasure-sucking which occupy the baby's mind, that is called 'narcissistic' choice, after the Greek myth of Narcissus who fell in love with his own reflection in a pool. In this case the child can love only himself, for his self grows around this first differentiation. To be more precise, he can love only himself or extensions or representations of himself in the world. A narcissistic man may love his country devotedly – because it is his country, himself writ large – and appear to have no self-love at all because he has emptied it on to this other self. A narcissistic woman may be very unselfish and modest about herself but inordinate in her conceits and ambitions for her children. A narcissist can only love what he can somehow connect with himself and then loves it because it is himself. Anaclitic love, true object-love, is free to love anything in the world. Whoever achieves it is not dependent on his own image to provoke his love. He has crossed the bridge from self to the world. He can love an object for its own sake, and not because it is part of him. Of course by his love for it he incorporates it into himself. The incorporation of the object into the self, or the extension of the self to the object – whichever way we look at it – is secondary in anaclitic love. It is primary in narcissism and love is secondary. Hence anaclitic love is freer and has a much wider choice of object.

It seems reasonable to suppose that the richer forms of personality depend upon anaclitic love and that failure to develop it is a maldevelopment. One sign is the fact that in a person where it is attained weakly, that is, with a strong strain of narcissism underlying partial anaclitic love, frustration and hardship tend to produce regression to complete narcissism. This would appear to be in line with other regressions under frustration where a more advanced form of development is always given up for a more primitive and infantile one. It would take us too far afield to discuss the possible causes why in any particular person narcissism should be chosen rather than object-love but it is obviously a subject of the utmost importance for all branches of education.

A possible confusion of thought should be noted here. Narcissism is not the same as egoism and object-love is different from altruism. Egoism is that character trait in which the individual seeks only his own welfare and advantage, pursues only what is to his own interest. It is selfishness. Its opposite is altruism, devotion to the interests of others, concern for their welfare, unselfishness. There is no element of libidinal pleasure, either sensual or aim-inhibited, in egoism or altruism. Narcissism and object-love, the other pair of opposites, are libidinal dispositions. They refer to the way the libido seeks its satisfactions and not to what may be of advantage for the self or the loved object. Conceit and infatuation are exaggerated manifestations of them. An egoist is not necessarily narcissistic. He may be, but on the other hand he may have genuine object-love. In that case he will seek to possess his love objects, to use them for his own enjoyment and satisfaction, with little thought for their advantage or pleasure. Similarly the altruist may be narcissistic or anaclitic in his libidinal development. The narcissistic altruist will get great pleasure out of helping other people and he will do it more for his own satisfaction than for the actual good it does. The altruist with object-love will get his chief pleasure from seeing others gain from his actions.

Christian love (*agape*, or *caritas*) is none of these precisely. Indeed it is very difficult to define and there is no general agreement about what it is. Some describe it almost in terms of altruisim – a rather conscientious altruism – as considered thoughtfulness for the welfare of other people, and make it more a matter of will than of emotion. On the other hand the fervent language of some of the mystics describing their feelings towards God or Christ uses terms that are almost directly lifted from the setting of intense erotic passion. No doubt Christian love as it is generally understood lies between these extremes. It is warmer than altruism and more disciplined than passion. It seems to be a blend of altruism, aim-inhibited object-love, or tender affection, and narcissism. In the fervent

THE BRIDGE TO THE WORLD

mystics, the sensual aim nearly breaks through the inhibition but is converted through symbolism into mystical passion. If the repression of love is severe we get the sterner, duty type of *agape*. The narcissism explains the inner exaltation of Christian love which is almost a sensual feeling of well-being, an uplifting of the self, an ecstasy of loving and being loved. Although this feeling is largely the expression of narcissism, there is another element in it which we are not yet ready to discuss, the close approximation of the Ego to the Ego-ideal.

It is rather surprising to find narcissism in Christian love, and it is not to be explained by saying that most Christians start off as narcissists, imperfectly developed personalities, and therefore carry their narcissism into their religion. Narcissism seems to belong intrinsically to *agape*. That surely is the meaning of Christ's teaching: 'Love thy neighbour as thyself.' Possibly it is explained by the fact that there are two grades of narcissism. The primary state of love in the infant is narcissism. This belongs to the period before there is any marked differentiation in its world of sensations into self and not-self. The choice we have spoken of between anaclitic and narcissistic love arises with the differentiation. Thus object or anaclitic love is a development out of primary narcissism. Secondary narcissism would be fixated narcissism. We therefore have two kinds of narcissism; this fixated narcissism and free narcissism which would be the primary reservoir of libido. In object-love the libido flows out from this storehouse and attaches itself to objects. That seems to be the normal life impulse. In secondary, fixated, narcissism it is inhibited from doing this, but attaches itself to the self instead. In certain conditions, such as tiredness and illness, it withdraws from the objects because the reservoir is getting exhausted and the life impulse weakens. In sleep the object cathexes are almost completely cut off, the mind has retreated from the world, the energy sinks back into the primary reservoir, and the cessation of output together with the normal creation of new energy builds up the supply again so that we wake with renewed energy and zeal to face the world. If it is this primary narcissism, as we may call it, that is involved in Christian love, and not the secondary fixated or regressive type, that would explain why Christian love finds great resources of power. Power is one of its characteristics.

Egoism, self-centredness, is the very antithesis of Christianity, and if it is magnified by secondary narcissism it produces an anti-social character that tends constantly to megalomania and cannot adapt itself to the requirements of normal life, a character that has no regard for the feelings or the welfare of other people and is in effect conscienceless. Cunning replaces reason, for the intellect is used as an instrument to further egoistic interests and justify narcissistic vanity. Unbridled egoism is the chief of the seven deadly sins.

It is interesting to note that Christianity offers hope of full development to both anaclitic object-love and narcissistic love. If they are caught up fully into Christian love they reach the same goal. Take the case of the narcissist. His narcissism prevents him at first from loving the world. He can only love that portion of it wherein in some fashion he sees himself. Christianity then says to him, 'You are a potential child of God, the world and the heavens are your home; be yourself.' It enlarges the concept of self so that in loving himself, he loves his fellow men and identifies his welfare with theirs until there is no limit to his love.

If, on the other hand, a person has crossed the bridge into object-love, the way is opened to him to pass on and love the whole world. Christianity offers the same scope to him, but it does not have to begin by showing him that the world is his home. It reaches him primarily by confronting him with a God at the heart of the world who is love, active love reaching out to him to confer its benefits on him. Once he has made contact with this love through meeting someone in whom it is embodied, his love is stimulated in return and grows to its fullness.

In neither case is the process to the final stage as easy or as simple as it may seem from this brief description, and we shall have to come back to it at a later point when we are considering the meaning of the Atonement in the light of psychoanalysis. We shall then see that in differing ways both types can find their way to the full realization of themselves through Christ.

Before we take up that question we have to look at various other considerations arising out of the stages of development of the young child's mind. And first of all is the point which begins this chapter, that the mother is the bridge by which the child crosses from self to the world. It is a very common occurrence for people to get stuck on the bridge and not go on, that is, they suffer from a mother-fixation. The metaphor is not very apt here, for in this as in most fixations there are degrees in which the libido is fixated. Even in the worst fixations probably some of the libido moves on, but it is disproportionately small compared with the requirements of healthy development. Moreover, the libido that is caught in the fixation is not as a rule entirely lost in the internal conflict for, as we have seen, much of it finds its way into action by means of displacements or sublimations.

Mother-fixations express themselves in an infinite variety of forms and of course tend to carry with them the prohibitions belonging to the repressions. For instance, they frequently cause unhappy marriages. A man may, under the influence of his unconscious, choose a wife in the image of his mother. The unconscious barriers against marrying his mother then operate against his wife and the marriage proves most unsuccessful. His marriage is too close to the unconscious wish to be freely allowed as a displacement. A common form of displacement of a mother-fixation is on to an abstract idea, or some impersonal symbol, and in various ways these can be served with all the devotion that is unconsciously given to the mother. Some of these symbols are easy to understand – Mother Earth, for instance. In a very obvious sense the earth is mother of us all. The ocean is also a mother symbol, especially in the unconscious. Byron expresses this very directly in his 'Apostrophe to the Ocean' in *Childe Harold*. Again, one's country can be a mother symbol – 'Mother India', '*la France*', 'Ireland', illustrate this. It is interesting in this connexion that Britain has had her two periods of greatest expansion under queens – Queen Elizabeth and Queen Victoria. The queen is almost inevitable as an unconscious mother symbol. It would be very interesting to examine why some countries become symbolized in paternal fashion – *Vaterland*, John Bull, Uncle Sam – and others in the maternal, and to trace the effects upon the character of the members of the different nations.

The mother symbol which most directly interests us in this study is the Church. Psychoanalysts tell us that in dreams a church is a common symbol of the mother, and there is no doubt too that the abstract idea of the Church is readily made a substitute for the mother. The New Testament uses the image of the Church as the bride of Christ, but even without that it seems inevitable that mother-fixations would easily be displaced on to the Church. We call her Mother Church. Some Christian denominations express the idea more openly than others, notably the Roman Catholics. I am not referring to the sense in which one Church gives birth to others, as the Church of England has founded branches in various parts of the world which have grown into independent Churches in full communion with the Mother Church in England. I am using the term to mean that individual members of the Churches have in their unconscious minds identified their Church with their mother. Their conscious minds may treat the name Mother Church as a metaphor, but in their unconscious it has psychical reality, that is, the Church is their mother. Those Christians who manifest a strong emotional anti-Papal bias, or who think of the Church of Rome as the 'scarlet woman', betray the unconscious mother-identification by their negative reaction. They resist the idea of the Father (the Pope) having power over the mother (the Church). Their 'Protestantism' is a reaction formation. Their reaction is against their repressed Oedipus Complex wishes and their intense emotional bias draws its strength from unconscious sources. Anti-Papal convictions that are based on reasoned judgements may show even greater tenacity, but they are not accompanied by the heat of violent emotion. In this, of course, they illustrate the way in which all beliefs arrived at by the reasoned judgements of the Ego have a different emotional quality from those which give expression to unconscious fixations.

Various consequences follow from the identification of the Church with the mother. The first of them is that the Church will always exercise an attraction for people with a strong mother-fixation, particularly an early one before the Oedipus Complex has reached its most acute phase. If jealousy of the father has entered into the fixation there may be an oscillation between attraction to the Church and repulsion from it. The attraction will be to the mother but the repulsion will be from God (the great father symbol), to whom the Church submits, or from the parson (another father-substitute) who is likely to be accused of dogmatism, of authoritarianism, of smugness, and other stupidities. The parson may indeed be guilty of all these, especially if he himself has a strong mother-fixation, for he has got into the position of the father, but he may be innocent and yet accused of them. We shall take up the theme of the father in the next chapter. It is mentioned here as a reminder that fixations operate at all stages and as a warning that behaviour is rarely the product of one simple motive but the confluence of many strands acting and interacting in a most complex way. It is necessary for the sake of exposition to deal as far as possible with one aspect at a time, but we must not expect to find it as simple as that in actual fact, where behaviour is prompted by many converging motives, conscious and unconscious, from different levels of the mind.

Those who are attracted to a Church because of their mother-fixation will adopt towards it an attitude corresponding to that of an infant in his earliest years. They will expect from it the fulfilment of all their desires for happiness. That in their minds is the chief *raison d'être* of the Church, a guarantee of a good time coming by and by if it can't be fulfilled now. They will expect comfort in trouble, as the infant runs crying to his mother to be petted and fussed over when hurt in any way. The Church will mean security and consolation, and above all it will be for them a haven of retreat from a hard world, a world which doesn't make things easy for you, where you suffer, and, worst of all, a world which doesn't treat you as of much significance. The infant basking in his mother's love feels that he is the most important and most valuable person in the world. He learns by a series of shocks that other people don't regard him as nearly so important as he believes he is and the temptation is to run away from this hurt to his egoism and narcissism, back to the warm, comforting, protecting love of the mother. That is just what many people seek in the Church – an escape from reality, from hardship and the need to overcome hurts and privation by effort. At this level it ties up closely with the return to the womb fantasy and tends to produce the same 'other-worldly' type of religion. As mother-fixation lies at the root of a great many major and minor neuroses we can expect to find a disproportionate number of moral weaklings in the congregations of the Churches, weaklings not necessarily in the sense that they are given to immoral habits, but rather that they are repressed, undeveloped and warped personalities, incapable of the creative efforts which a full life demands of them. Their virtues are negative ones. They endure pain and hardship patiently, not victoriously using it as a stepping stone to something greater. It is a paradox that the Christian Church should thus attract and, it must be said, often encourage the kind of person who is the very reverse of Christ, fearless, independent, strong and creative.

Where it is the clergy who are afflicted with a mother-fixation, their tendency is likely to be to put the Church in the foreground of their teaching rather than God, to deify it. They defend the Church against all attack, all criticism and, sometimes, all change. Worship will tend to be made as sensual as possible, not merely in language but by every means available, light and colour, sound and scent, ceremony and gesture. In this way the repressed sensual devotion to the mother gets displaced expression on the mother symbol, the Church. A very strong mother-fixation may produce just the opposite by reaction-formation, a violent aversion from such beliefs and practices, for the reason that indulgence in them tends to bring the repressed mother-fixation too close to the surface and rouses the repressing forces to react and drive the Ego to move too far in the opposite direction.

We may ask whether there is any value in such mother-substitute religion. The full answer cannot be given till we are in a position to draw all the diverse threads together, but there are three considerations to note here. In the first place, it is not the religion of Christ. We could not expect it to be, for Christ showed no signs of a mother-fixation, but had completely resolved his Oedipus Complex, not merely as a child, but in his sublimest relations with God the Father. The danger is that it may and certainly does in many instances prevent growth into true Christianity. It is a form of fantasy life, not reality living. In the second place, there are a great many people who suffer from this maldevelopment of personality whom we cannot expect to be cured. Even if they knew they were psychologically abnormal the practical opportunities of treatment are not open to them. Indeed, they have more chance of being cured through Christianity than elsewhere. But if they cannot be cured they must find some release and the Church provides the means of using their devotion in social service and other socially useful ways. Thus their substitute satisfactions for their unconscious mother-fixations not only give them pleasure but are turned to the help of other people. Everyone who has anything to do with a church congregation knows how much hard, self-sacrificing, patient work is done by such people, whose only reward is to feel they are serving the Church and have a place in it. The third point to note is that sometimes the displacement may become a real sublimation, and an enduring happiness and stability of personality be found. This is perhaps more likely to happen through the Church than through other forms of displacement, though one cannot dogmatize on the matter. In these cases freedom has been achieved and it seems very likely that people who find stability and happiness and freedom through conversion to Christianity after lives of conflict and mental torment – and there are many outstanding examples of this – have not merely found in religion a substitute satisfaction for their repressed wishes but have sublimated them permanently and really found freedom. In his Epistles it is the note of freedom that St Paul most emphasized. St Paul, however, seems to have been struggling with repressions concerning the father rather than the mother, but the possibilities hold for mother-fixations too.

To end the chapter we must look at the significance of the Church as mother symbol for those who do go on beyond the mother to the fullness of reality and grow up psychologically.

Going on beyond the mother means being weaned psychologically as well as physically from her, and of the two the psychological weaning is much the more difficult. It is as hard for the mother to relinquish her child emotionally as it is for the child to win to independence. But just as the mother gradually trains her baby to take other and more solid and varied food than her milk, so she must help him to find other interests and other love objects than herself until he wins to complete independence from her. The parallel does not hold strictly, because in physical weaning the infant gives up the mother's breast completely, whilst in the psychological she remains always an important object of love. But his love is not tied to her. In actual fact, if his love is freed, he is able to love her more as a real person and not as a mental image constructed out of the unreal fantasies of the infantile mind, an idealization out of all relation to the actual mother. A mother-fixation not only involves the prohibitions and repressions which hinder the expression of love towards the mother, but the real mother may be starved of love because it is all poured on to the unconscious mother image and may be displaced anywhere but on the mother herself.

The mother thus plays a part of incomparable importance in the mental life of a child in addition to her biological function. By her care and love for him she first gives him the sense of security and of worth that he needs at the beginning of his life. Then without ceasing to love him or repudiating his love, she encourages his independence and sets him free from her, and herself from him, until the final result is seen in his going off to found a family of his own with his own mate. Thus from his first touch with the world through his mother's breast, he has been led on through her to the whole world in which his life is lived. She is the prototype of reality for him and it is inevitable that he should expand his image of her to include the world; Mother Earth, Mother Ocean, Mother Land, Mother Church, all have grown out of her. The danger only comes when they are a symbol or substitute for her and not a development from her.

It is more than an analogy to call the Church Mother. It is also reasonable to suppose that the Church should treat her children in the way equivalent to that of the mother who sets her children free of infantile bondage to herself. Her aim should be to give them freedom and independence, to pass them on to the world to face its dangers, its frustrations and its challenges and to surmount them. If the Church tries to hold her children or to protect them from the trials and hardships, the temptations and struggles of the world, she is simply repeating the behaviour of the family mother who crippled the development of her children by mother-fixation. The Church, therefore, must be a training ground for spiritual life, not an overriding authority. She must train her children to rely upon themselves, under God, and not seek to hold them to herself in fear that they may go astray. The consequence of such an attitude on her part would be the same as that which follows from similar behaviour by the family mother – namely, increased love and stronger family relationships. Too often, however, the Church has seen her function as that of imposing her authority over her members, of disciplining them, of prescribing how they must behave, of giving them rules of belief and conduct which they must not question. She may succeed, but at the cost of halting their growth to the fullness of personality, to the 'fullness of the stature of Christ'.

To sum up. The Church takes over in religious development the functions of the mother and does so in a real sense psychologically. The relationship of the child with the mother may be a grave impediment to growth, for it may result in a mother-fixation. This mother-fixation becomes repressed and frequently gets its substitute expression by displacement upon the Church. The result is a religion of fantasy, the satisfaction of unconscious wishes. But in any case the mother is the most important early factor in the child's life, the only bridge by which he can escape from fantasy to the real world. So if she is the good mother who sets her child free and helps him to grow in independence and self-reliance, she enables him at the same time to find in the Church the same source of growth and strength for his spiritual life. The good Church must have the same characteristics as the good family mother.

CHAPTER 9

GOD – THE FATHER

NEXT to the mother in importance in the development of the child is the father. The mother is the bridge to the world, the father is the road to God for him. As might be expected, the steps are complicated and the journey to the proper destination by no means sure. Fixations and complexes develop in the relations of the infant with his father and these express themselves in religious or pseudo-religious behaviour, as any other unconscious tendency does. A perpetual task confronting the student of the bases of religion is to discriminate between behaviour that is the product of abnormal development and that which is the outcome of free growth through the successive stages of normal development. As belief in God is the essential core of religion, except in pure Buddhism, which dispenses with gods, we need to exercise the utmost care in disentangling the various threads which go to make up that belief. That is, we must see the different roles played by the father and the father-image in the life of the child. This holds true of Christianity.

Perhaps this is the right point to raise a matter which has only had passing mention before. It has to do with the composition of the father-image and of the mother-image as well. I have spoken as though the psychic image of each of the parents was derived from the actual father and mother respectively. This is not strictly true. In each case the image is a compound of both parents in the infant's mind. One reason for this derives from the bi-sexual nature of human beings. Every individual is a combination of masculine and feminine elements or tendencies. No one is absolute male or female in psychological make-up. When therefore in the previous chapter, we spoke of the role played by the mother, it would have been more correct to speak of the compound mother-image (of which the mother is the representative or focus) derived from the feminine elements in both father and mother. It is true that the mother's breast is the first contact with reality, but the father does not suddenly enter the child's consciousness as a separate person; he is differentiated out from the mother by slow degrees. In the process, his feminine qualities are blended with those of the mother in the psychical mother-image which the infant forms. Similarly, the masculine elements of the mother find a place in the father-image.

We have seen that in the case of the mother, the infant forms an idealized picture of her, based upon his infantile attachments to her and his dependence on her, and that this image may remain unaltered in his unconscious. So too, the father-image is never a replica of the actual father, but is a product of the infant's relations with the father. It too may be repressed and remain unaltered in the unconscious throughout life. In normal development, however, the image of each parent is gradually modified and corrected as the child grows older and his position relative to his father and mother changes. He becomes less helpless, less directly dependent on them, is more able to meet them as an equal personality with opinions of his own, and he has also widened his knowledge of people so that he can judge them not only in relation to himself but in comparison with other men and women. He is able to form a realistic picture of them which replaces the fantasy image of the infantile period. Even if the infantile image was repressed the later conscious estimate will still be formed, though it will be liable to distortion under the influence of the repressed image, and the two will co-exist in the mind, one on the unconscious level, the other on the conscious.

A further complication arises from the illogical character of unconscious thinking. The unconscious does not obey the laws of logic which classifies, associates and integrates ideas according to general principles of meaning. The conscious mind cannot hold contradictory ideas together at the same time except under the influence of the unconscious, but to the unconscious this is an everyday happening. Thus, instead of one father- or mother-image there may be several, all different, even violently contradictory. There is a common tendency to split the mother-image into the good and bad mothers – the idealized woman and the loose woman. This may have disastrous results in later life. But it can also profoundly affect other aspects of life. It can work through the developments we have seen in the last chapter and bring about corresponding complications of belief and behaviour according to whether the good- or bad-mother image is dominant in the particular expression. Reluctantly, we must put this fascinating topic aside and consider the part played by the father-image in the psychological phenomena of religion. There can be a good-father image, a loving, protecting, gift-bringing father, and a bad-father image who seeks to destroy, who imposes his will by violence, who watches every move in the hope of finding reason to attack. The consequences of splitting the image into a good father and a bad father will become clear as we proceed.

The infant's relations with the father have not the same immediacy as those with the mother. The mother is distilled out of himself, as it were, when he becomes aware of distinctions within the mass of sensations which form his life in the early period. The father is separated out from the mother, not from himself, and he therefore always has the character of 'otherness', of externality. In the same way, when grown up he will ascribe to God that 'otherness'. God is remote, transcendent, 'wholly other', what Otto called a 'mysterium', something not intrinsically knowable. The father must have for the infant the same characteristics as Otto found in the 'mysterium' — namely 'tremendum' and 'fascinans'. He overawes and fascinates the infant. In the presence of the father he feels weak and helpless, a small thing of no account. He believes the father is all-powerful and as a small boy proudly boasts of the prowess of his father. The mother, of course, first plays the role of protector and comforter and bringer of food to the infant, but once the father is clearly differentiated out from her, this role is transferred to him. We must remember that the first impressions of the infant are formed within the narrowest of family circles and there are no standards in that by which to compare him and so no apparent limits to what the father can do. He is strong and can therefore protect in case of danger. He is the great hero to be admired and imitated, the ideal of manhood, the acme of perfection, all that one could desire to be. He is the master of the family and the supplier of all things. This image of the father formed in the early period of the infant's knowledge of him is the prototype and origin of the idea of God the Creator.

But the father appears in another guise. He is the source of authority. In actual fact, discipline and control may be administered by the mother, but even the most hen-pecked and subservient father appears to the infant as the one who wields authority. The infant's narcissism combined with his desire to be loved by the mother and his love for the pleasures he gets from her make him believe that she loves him before anything else. It is not possible for him at this stage to conceive of her loving anyone else. This precludes him from believing that she would punish him or deny him anything of her own free will, so anything she does to restrain him or punish him must be, in his mind, because she is under the power of the father. He cannot doubt her love for him. The father, then, appears to the child as the imposer of restrictions and as the instigator of frustrations. Even the failure to attain some of his wishes which are physically impossible, crying for the moon, may be ascribed to him, for the infant has no conception as yet of the nature of physical impossibility. His outlook is animistic, and frustration is explicable only in animistic terms as the effect of ill will, ill will on the part of the father so far as the infant is concerned. Thus, in its first beginning, authority comes as denying the satisfaction of desire. It is negative, prohibiting, expressing itself as 'thou shalt not'. This picture of the father is held alongside the earlier one without any necessary assimilation or adjustment to remove the contradictions. Complete synthesis of ideas is a very mature form of mental functioning. It is very common, almost universal, even in adults, to hold conflicting ideas without seeing their contradiction because they are never brought together. They are kept in a state of dissociation. The reason for this usually, if not always, is that they embody repressions, and the unconscious, being derived from the infantile mind, is not troubled by considerations of logical consistency. Its criterion of importance is emotional significance. It should not puzzle us, therefore, to find divergent ideas about the father, held simultaneously by the infant. The child that can hate and rage at his father at one moment can be filled with love and admiration for him a minute later as a result of a new emotional interest developing.

In his book *Totem and Taboo*, Freud develops an extremely interesting theory of the origins of human society in prehistory when man had barely emerged from the animal stage. It is an illuminating theory and repays careful study. It is certainly rich in suggestiveness for understanding certain aspects of the human mind and its functioning, not least in the sphere of religion. We cannot even summarize here the main conclusions he comes to, let alone the evidence in support, but one aspect of it is closely related to what we have been considering about the infant's formation of a father-image. Freud does not base his psychological theories on this venture into prehistory. The essay is an exploration of a sociological field to see what evidence exists there to illustrate and confirm conclusions firmly based on other evidence of a more accurate and precise nature. Freud accepts the Darwinian hypothesis of a primal horde of women and young males ruled over by the brute strength of the father. The latter is absolute despot knowing no law but his own will. If any of the males tries to usurp his privileges and possess the females, he attacks them and kills them, or drives them off, or reduces them to abject submission. Those who were driven off no doubt tried to capture females from the horde or other hordes to set up groups of their own. Those who remained did so on the condition of controlling and repressing their desires towards their father's wives. The repressed libido is diverted to strengthen the homosexual aim-inhibited ties between the brothers and bind them into a unity. United they are able to do what singly they had all wanted to do but had lacked the power to carry out. They kill the father. The father dead, the brothers no doubt fought among themselves to possess the spoils, until one of them conquered or the horde broke up. This must have happened countless times until the brothers learned not to fight among themselves after killing the primal father. They remained united, but the only condition on which they could do so was to continue to accept the veto imposed by the father during his lifetime. The women of the horde – or tribe as it becomes – are taboo to them and they seek their wives from outside groups. The dead father is as powerful as he was when alive. He endures in their minds as an idea, an image or a symbol, imposing the unbreakable laws. He is the totem of the tribe figured as its animal ancestor. In symbolizing the primal father as an animal the primitive mind was only doing what is constantly done by the unconscious in dreams.

In some such way as this the primal-father image persisting in the minds of the males of the tribe became the source of tribal law and psychologically was the chief instrument in enforcing it. But before the arbitrary will of the horde father was transmuted into accepted law, and before cohesive society could be established, the libidinal desires of the males had to be subjected to severe repression, repression that was later maintained by the preservation of the primal father as a mental image represented by the totem of the tribe. There is another feature in the killing of the primal father, the eating of him which is regularly renewed in the totem feast, which we shall take up in a later chapter in connexion with the sacrament of communion which is the central act of Christian worship.

Freud suggests that the primal-father image has become embodied in the inherited structure of the mind as at least a nucleus upon which the real-father image is built during the lifetime of the individual. Whether this is so or not has not been established but the theory of the primal father corresponds very closely with what happens in the development of the mind through the Oedipus Complex.

We have seen how the infantile sex instincts come to their culmination in the phallic stage, and in the case of the boy – to which for the sake of simplicity we have mainly to confine this study – in an intense desire to possess the mother and oust the father. This is a revival of the primal father situation, except that the little boy cannot pretend even to the strength and size necessary to challenge the father. The wish felt by the boy has psychical reality, that is, in his mind he is as guilty as if he had actually carried the wish into action. This psychical reality of wishes is a feature of the unconscious that we have already noted. Further, the boy, possessed by the desire to destroy or get rid of the father, projects the desire on to him and so believes that the father wants to get rid of him, or to castrate him by cutting off his penis, which he has come to feel as the central organ of his love for the mother. The dream which I used to illustrate this phase of the Oedipus Complex reveals the primal father idea – the fantasy of the terrifying, destructive father avenging the infringement of his prerogatives. We saw then that the normal outcome of the Oedipus Complex was for the boy to introject the father-image. The process, if we may repeat, was as follows. The boy identifies himself with the father. This he can do because of two things: first, his positive love for him, which makes him want to be in the closest relations with the father, to do everything he can to win and retain his love, to be like him, to set him up as hero and ideal; secondly, because the father is in the position he himself would like to be, as the possessor of the loved woman, and so by imagining that he is the father he can get a vicarious satisfaction of his wishes.

By identifying himself with the father he creates a division within his Ego. The father-identification sets itself over against the self-ego, the executive Ego developed to carry out in the real world the impulses from the Id, and it becomes for that self-ego both an ideal to be striven after and a source of authority repeating the commands of the father from within the mind. This father-identification establishes itself as the Super-ego, the source of inner commands, censorship, standards. In its aspect of being a positive ideal of what the little boy wants to become – strong and wise like his father – it is the Ego-ideal. Henceforth the Super-ego supervises all the actions of the Ego in its dealings with the Id. Since the infant's picture of the father is of an omniscient, omnipotent being, the Ego offers an unconditional obedience to the Super-ego. Herein lies the source of the 'categorical imperative', the absolute 'ought' of duty, which is made the basis of most systems of ethics. It is thus the seat of conscience. The 'ought' which conscience imposes as an ideal of conduct is the internal pressure exerted by the Super-ego on the Ego when the Ego has tentatively accepted and is about to carry into action some impulse from the Id which is contrary to the standards of the Super-ego. These standards do not remain at the level of moral understanding attained by the infant at the age of five to seven years, the age at which he should have achieved this resolution of the Oedipus Complex. Around the central core of the Super-ego constituted by the introjected father-image are gathered all the moral standards acquired during life from home, school, Church, sport, nation and other sources. They are assimilated to the early ideal and are given the absolute authority which it has, the authority derived from the infant's acceptance of the absolute power of the father.

In the next chapter we shall take further the question of the meaning of conscience and the unconditional 'ought' of morals in the light of this analysis of its structure. The rest of this chapter must be devoted to the general idea of God. We have seen earlier in the chapter how special forms of the father-image can be reflected in the character we ascribe to God, but we have not yet seen how the idea of God is directly developed from the image of the father.

None of us creates the idea of God for himself. We each acquire it from the society in which we live. A study of the origin of the idea would therefore involve a full and comprehensive analysis of the history of human life and thought. We cannot undertake that. We do not need to. We can at this point simply consider the psychological function of the idea of God in the human mind. It is safe to say that no idea persists as a continuing force unless it serves some human need that cannot find adequate satisfaction in some other way, or unless it corresponds to an objective reality which is observable, measurable, or can be inferred by reason from observable phenomena and can be applied to produce predictable results. This table before me is observable. The law of gravity is inferable and from it predictions can be made which are verifiable by observation. But inference is notoriously unreliable as a guide to conclusions and the field within which it gives sound results is much more limited than we are prone to believe, because we are under the dazzlement of the spotlight thrown on the physical sciences. In ordinary life we are only too familiar with the way reasoning regularly leads us to the conclusions we wish to reach. We take only selected facts, we introduce false premises, or we overlook false reasoning. In passing we may note that even trained scientists are susceptible to these weaknesses outside their own special fields.

Now we can admit at once that God is not an observable or measurable phenomenon. The language of religion may sometimes give the impression of claiming that He is, but I do not think that many Christians would attempt to substantiate such a claim. Our belief in His existence, therefore, is due either to inference from the nature of various facts which can be observed or it is purely a creation of the mind projected upon the world to suit our emotional and instinctive needs, but having no objective basis. In the latter case the idea of God might be inevitable, in the sense that men cannot help constructing it because of the inner working of their minds. If that were the sole reason why men actually do believe in God, we should still have to take the belief seriously. But Christianity firmly and emphatically claims that certain facts can only be explained on the hypothesis that God exists and that He has a character of love, best symbolised by calling Him Father.

I have already said that I believe this claim of Christianity is true and that it is beside the aim of this book to prove the truth of such a claim. Most Christians who believe in the existence of God do not do so because they have first examined the arguments to prove it. They accept the idea because it satisfies a psychological need and it is only later, if at all, that they critically examine the reasons in support of the belief. It does not necessarily follow that the idea is false because it comes to the individual in this way, since behind the form in which it is presented to him there lies a great deal of history of thought and experience. It does mean, however, that the individual is likely to interpret the idea in a way adapted to his unconscious thinking, that he is likely to be exposed in his thinking about God to the influence of his repressed infantile father-images. To put it more precisely, he will accept the idea of God in a form determined by patterns which are derived unconsciously from the father-image. He cannot do anything else. We can only assimilate and interpret new experiences, new ideas, by assimilating them to previous experience, and in the case of the idea of God as it is normally presented nothing else is so relevant as the early relations with the father. We have seen, for instance, that the infant sees the father as his protector and believes him infinitely wise and strong, giving the comfort of security and freedom from anxiety to the helpless infant. He will likewise find this in God.

The world does not grow easier as we grow older. Increasing knowledge and strength bring with them more complex and more difficult problems. Insecurity and danger of different kinds hang over us: sickness, accident, unemployment, loneliness, bereavement, frustration, failure, war and above all inescapable death. By growing up, man does not escape from the helplessness of infancy. That helplessness is transferred to a wider sphere. He therefore unconsciously seeks to recreate the security he drew in infancy from the possession of an all-powerful protecting father. He tries to find a father in the universe and interprets every sign he can as evidence of such an almighty father's existence. He projects the image of the father upon the universe and makes a picture of God, who protects him from danger, supplies him with the animals of the chase or the fruits of the earth, gives him victory in war, and prolongs his life after death.

God thus offers security and protection against the uncertainties, the sufferings, the hardships of the world in the face of which we feel helpless. The more difficult life becomes the more we tend to cling to a belief in God as our mainstay. One only needs to think of favourite hymns to realize how widespread this attitude is. Whatever may be the reasonable factual justification for such a belief in God, it is a psychological necessity for the infantile type of mind. It is in this sense that Freud calls religion an 'illusion', the creation of a wish. We need not go so far as Freud, who implies that it is probably only that, but we must accept the fact that wish-fulfilment must play a large part in shaping the ideas of God we hold. We must make allowance for it and be on the watch to discern what is purely subjective from what is based on objective reasons, and also, a point which we shall later see as of great importance, what is abnormal, infantile, repressed, fixated, from what is normal, adult and free. It may be inevitable that almost everyone first accepts and interprets the idea of God by way of wish-fulfilment. It is not necessary that the belief remain on this level. Indeed, healthy religion will aim to take its adherents beyond it. It will grow beyond the infantile to the adult. Thus belief in God may give us confidence and peace because in the face of the overpowering difficulties of life we regress to infantile helplessness and we need the sense of the father's protection. Such peace and confidence will betray other infantile characteristics, notably that it is egocentric, and we can best recognize its true character in that way. The true 'peace of God' does not confer protection. It gives strength and comes from accepting hardship and danger, and its distinguishing mark is that it shows a freely expressed love and service of other people.

In projecting the father upon the world and arriving at the idea of God, the unconscious does not carry over only the protecting father. We have seen that the father is also a source of danger to the infant. In the same way that the protective character of the father enters into the idea of God, so does the danger from the father. He first appears as frustrating the wishes of the infant and imposing an arbitrary authority upon him to which obedience is compelled by his absolute power. This negative conception of the father is reflected in the attitude to God which sees Him as the author of prohibitive commands constituting a negative morality. In this guise God is the watchful eye always on the alert to forbid us doing what we want to do and ordering us to do things for which we have little desire. He is pictured as the watchful censor, taking the joy out of life and always ready to punish us for transgressing His hard will. Morality of this type means unquestioning obedience to an external authority called the will of God, which is of an arbitrary character and to be obeyed because God imposes it and punishes transgression. God is, as it were, the enemy. His harshness is no doubt mitigated by His 'mercy', in that He rewards obedience by acceptance into His favour, which is in some way inexpressible bliss. But He is a very hard taskmaster, counting every transgression against us, even visiting the sins of the fathers upon the children, grandchildren and great-grandchildren. In His eyes we are so bad that there would be no hope of escaping His everlasting wrath if it weren't that His Son is on our side and, by accepting punishment for our sins while himself innocent, satisfies the demands of God and procures pardon for us. This is the religion of Hell fire, of everlasting damnation, of a God jealous of His rights and His honour, exacting every ounce of homage and obedience from worthless man; religion much more occupied with sin than with love. I shall say nothing here of the Devil or Satan to whom unrepentant sinners are handed over for punishment. He is a projection of the bad-father image. Belief in the Devil makes belief in a good God psychologically easier – though possibly more difficult logically.

It might appear at first sight that the mature mind should outgrow these infantile creations of God on the pattern of the father-image and arrive at a position of atheism. But atheism is not a sign of maturity. It is also the repetition of an infantile situation. The young child jealous of his father, fearing him, and resenting the frustrations which he imposes by command or by the simple fact of being what he is, wishes to get rid of his father, that is, wishes he were not there at all. When he is a few years older this may take the form of defiance or rebellion against the father. Many boys leave home at the earliest chance. Others defy the father and flout his authority in special ways, such as, for instance, in the choice of a profession or political party. Atheism is the projection of the wish that the father should be non-existent. It gets rid of the father by getting rid of God. In such cases we should expect to find that the father has crept back in some other form, most commonly in the unquestioning acceptance of some human authority – a thinker or political leader. And atheism will also tend to betray its infantile origin by its preoccupation in a negative way with the idea of God. We see this very clearly in the zeal of so many so-called 'rationalists'. They seem to spend more time arguing about the non-existence of God than most believers give to thoughts of His existence.

Normal growth of the mind leads neither to the continuance of those beliefs about God which are the unconscious projection of repressed infantile images of the father, nor to atheism which is resistance to belief in God due to repressed wishes to dispense with the father, wishes equally infantile. Because the human mind is inevitably shaped, determined in its form, by the relations with the father, it is predisposed to interpret the universe according to the child-mother-father pattern, in which God plays the part of father. It may even be that a fully mature mind free from serious fixations and repressions will inevitably believe in God – though any belief in God does not of itself argue such maturity, for it is the character of the belief that is all-important. Whether this be so or not, belief in God, or disbelief in God, must be the product of minds that have passed successfully through the infantile stages of development, if it is to be regarded as healthy and mature. Just as the growing child has to solve his relations with his father to achieve his mental and emotional freedom and independence, so the believer must carry that same development into his attitude towards the God in whom he believes. What that implies will be examined more fully in the next three chapters.

CHAPTER 10

CONSCIENCE AND MORAL
OBLIGATION

THE resolution of the Oedipus Complex by which the young boy comes to terms with his father brings him, as we have seen, under the sway of morality, which is in the process usually linked with God. Psychoanalysis throws a great deal of light on the nature and functioning of conscience. Common Christian teaching on the subject tends to make conscience the core of religion and to repeat the dictum of Bishop Butler that 'conscience is the voice of God in the soul.' While that may have been intended more as a metaphor than a definition, it expresses a commonly held point of view that conscience is in some way transcendent in its functioning, that it is a divinely implanted guide to what is right and wrong and derives its authority from this divine source. It is recognized, of course, that men may and do act against what their consciences dictate, and this is regarded as sinful. It is also acknowledged that conscience can be blunted, or in extreme cases atrophied, and this is usually explained as the result of persistent sin, that is, refusing to do what conscience says is the right thing. Accordingly, many preachers who set out to foster a religious sense in men make their first step an attempt to stir up the consciences of such sinners and revive in them a 'sense of sin'.

The justification for this conception is that conscience seems to carry its own authority with it. It speaks to us not of what is reasonable or advantageous, but as imposing an obligation upon us to follow what it prescribes. It declares what we 'ought' to do. It sets before us a judgement in terms of 'right' and 'wrong' and declares that it is our unconditional 'duty' to do what is right, and refrain from what is wrong. It is more than a mere impulse or appetition towards a particular line of conduct, such as we experience, say, in the impulse towards eating when we are hungry or of running away when afraid. Those impulses may compete with others and we can submit them to tests other than that of strength and pass judgement upon them accordingly. In contrast, conscience carries a feeling of absoluteness, of finality, and does not accept any other standards as valid against it. It implies that we must accept, and that we have accepted, its dictates as binding upon us. It is this absolute, final quality about it, this unconditional obligation, that leads people to regard conscience as the supreme religious organ of the mind.

There are three facts which should cause us to hesitate before giving unqualified acceptance to this point of view. In the first place, men do not always act according to the direction of their conscience. In conventional terms, they sin. To explain this, theologians declare that man is by nature sinful, or at least prone to sin, that he inherits, as part of his make-up, something called original sin, from which he can only be freed by the grace of God which comes to him in various ways. Man therefore is a dualistic creature. He has a power – through the divinely implanted (perhaps even divinely operated) conscience – to discern what he ought to do, but the sin in him prevents his doing it until he is released from this second part of his nature by the grace of God. If conscience is what it is commonly believed to be, this seems the only explanation for the indisputable facts of men's disobedience to it and the holy lives some people achieve.

The second fact to note is the wide discrepancy between the actual behaviour dictated by the conscience of different people in similar circumstances. It used to be the custom, I understand, among the Fijian Islanders that properly brought up sons would put their parents to death, to save them from misery, when they grew aged and infirm. A son who failed in this 'humanitarian' duty would be very much a sinner and his conscience would no doubt prick him badly. The conscience of a Christian would dictate far different conduct. This is an extreme case, but the existence of such divergences forces some compromise on the 'voice-of-God' theorists. So the obligation attaching to a conscientious judgement is regarded as the divine element, but the differing prescriptions are explained as due to the fact that sin has blunted and distorted the working of conscience – therefore, we may note, making it an unreliable guide to right action – or else a more radical step is taken and the content of the judgements is seen to be the result of education, direct and indirect. Once this view is fully admitted not much remains of 'divine' conscience.

The third fact to be noted, and it is probably the most significant, is that in young children we find only a rudimentary conscience, operating in ways that differ from an adult's conscience, and that we can trace fairly easily how it develops and becomes transformed into the latter. This is largely due to the understanding of the child mind that psychoanalysis has brought. But by the 'voice-of-God' theory, with its corollary of the blunting effect of sin, we should expect to find in the young child a clearly developed conscience working with great clarity and power. Instead, as William James pointed out in his classic work on psychology, the young healthy child is a pagan, seemingly lacking in any moral sense. His description has been amply confirmed by subsequent investigators. Further, if we find in young children a seemingly well-developed moral scrupulosity, instead of praising it we have reason now to suspect it as a sign of incipient neurosis. The veil of innocence with which adults are prone to cloak the doings of childhood has been ruthlessly torn aside and little children seen as committing or wishing to commit every crime in the calendar and doing it without compunction.

It has been recognized that conscience is a mode of mental functioning which is developed in the course of growth, and not a faculty fully operative from infancy; but it was not till Freud's work on the relations of Ego, Id and Super-ego that the true nature of conscience could be understood. Previous attempts to explain its genesis in the course of mental growth usually broke down because they could not give an adequate account of the peculiar quality of obligation attaching to conscience-judgements. They could not satisfactorily explain how various forms of pressure which are brought to bear by the social environment on the growing child to induce him to conform to the set standards of conduct are transformed into or replaced by the inward pressure of conscience using a unique form of compulsion.

This point was solved by Freud's description of the processes leading to the formation of the Super-ego. We have already discussed these in previous chapters, so it is only necessary to recapitulate the main points with whatever supplementary details may have special bearing on the question of conscience.

In the first place, Freud suggests that we probably inherit a rudimentary conscience. This is not, however, to be pictured in the traditional way as a special organ or faculty alongside others, but means that the complex structure of Id, Ego and Super-ego is present in outline from birth. Conscience is one aspect of the interplay of these. The developed Super-ego is chiefly the result of the introjection of the father-image, but Freud thinks that the long period in prehistory, when human society was evolving through the primal father stage, has left its mark on the mind in a kind of racial memory, by which he means more than a simple predisposition to the formation of conscience. He has not developed this suggestion very far, because if there is such an inheritance it is no more than rudimentary and not of great importance in itself in explaining conduct compared with the effects of developments in the lifetime of the individual.

The Super-ego is fully developed through the resolution of the Oedipus Complex by the introjection of the father-image (representative of both parents) to form a division within the Ego. The external authority of the father is thus transplanted into the self by an act of acceptance which gives the Super-ego its unique power to exact unquestioning obedience. The alternative in the fantasies of the infant was annihilation through castration. The existence of the Super-ego, therefore, implies that its authority has been acknowledged. On behalf of the Id the Ego may struggle against the exacting demands of the Super-ego and frequently succeeds in disobeying its behests. In so doing, it automatically brings on itself the condemnation of the Super-ego, which it feels as guilt. It cannot escape this feeling of guilt, for it is inevitably linked to the Super-ego. The Ego, however, can repress it into the unconscious, seeking to escape its paralysing and painful effects. It will also be remembered that the roots of the Super-ego are in the unconscious because it inherits from the Oedipus Complex and therefore functions in the unconscious as well as in consciousness. In the unconscious the Super-ego will meet and condemn impulses from the Id which never become conscious. Repression by the Super-ego at this level prevents them from doing so. These impulses, which are often expressed in unconscious fantasies, usually are intimately connected with the Oedipus Complex. The Super-ego's attack on them is felt as guilt. Sometimes the feeling of guilt enters consciousness, but usually it remains unconscious, like the repression which produces it. One of the major obstacles with which an analyst has to contend in his patients is the unconscious sense of guilt which sets up a strong resistance to being uncovered.

The image of the father that is introjected is not necessarily an accurate representation of the actual father. It is far more likely to reflect the violence of the boy's libidinal wishes, for it is that which determines how severe must be the restraints put upon them. It is therefore quite likely that an over-indulgent father may produce a strong Super-ego in the son. Yet it is also possible that severity of paternal discipline will contribute to a stern and exacting Super-ego.

There is another element in the Super-ego which was briefly noted in an earlier chapter, but which is of considerable importance in studying the working of the Super-ego. Mention of it gives me an opportunity to correct any false impression which may have arisen from the drastic simplification forced on us by the narrow limits of this brief study. I have been trying to present a very general picture of mental development and, while I have hinted at the extreme complexity of the mind, I have been forced to ignore much that throws light on the processes leading up to its final shape, much too that provides scope for wide deviations from normal development. I have given a schematic outline rather than an exact statement with all the qualifications and possible combinations of factors it would have involved. I have therefore hitherto neglected the early phases of the Super-ego, and of the Oedipus Complex, before the genital stage. From the view-point of psychology this is a cardinal omission, but perhaps it is not so vital, important as it still is, in our effort to trace the general contribution of psychoanalysis to the understanding of religion. My justification for the omission is that it requires an advanced knowledge of psychoanalysis to understand the theory of this section and I am debarred from presuming that or attempting to supply it. I can, therefore, only refer those who are interested to the relevant works on the subject (particularly to Melanie Klein's great study, *The Psychoanalysis of Children*).

Without, therefore, explaining the grounds on which the view is held, and using the most general terms, we can describe this third element in the Super-ego as coming from the development of the aggressive instincts in the period between birth and the resolution of the Oedipus Complex. The aggressive instincts begin to manifest themselves clearly in the secondary oral phase, the phase of biting which succeeds the sucking activity of the first six months. Biting gives the first opportunity of active destruction. The helplessness of the young child should not blind us to its aggressiveness. In fact it is that very helplessness which tends to promote it. The infant has strong instinctual needs for food, warmth, attention, but is helpless to control the world from which it must get its satisfactions. When it is frustrated it is thrown into a state of tension which soon overflows into anxiety. The anxiety is a threat to the Ego, which can only react by an attack upon the object. Some of the libidinal cathexis is diverted into aggressive rage, thus relieving the pressure, but there is also a proportion of pure aggression. The aggressiveness itself constitutes a danger to the Ego by its violence and because it may provoke reprisals (or so the infant fancies) from the objects attacked. To control the aggression the aggressive forces are themselves split and one part directed against the other to restrain it. It is also used to control the libido. This controlling element of aggression constitutes an early phase of the Super-ego. It can be very violent, particularly if the infant has had severe libidinal frustrations through, say, feeding difficulties.

There is little or no moral content in the Super-ego at this stage. That comes later with the resolution of the Oedipus Complex. In the young infant the Super-ego is simply a psychological device by which the self is able to gain a measure of self-control. But from this early development the Super-ego derives much of the severity with which in later periods it controls the Ego and the Id. In other words an acute conscience may be the sign not of a saintly disposition, but of feeding troubles in infancy. That is a possibility that we must recognize. To see its implications we must see the relations between conscience and the Super-ego and conscience and moral judgement.

Conscience is seated in the Super-ego and so are moral judgements – if for the moment we may treat them as different from conscience – but the function of the Super-ego is not primarily moral. It is a device developed by the mind to protect the Ego from dangers arising from excessive libido or aggression. In the earliest period of infancy it has this character almost solely, and that is why we find in infants up to two or three years of age, and even up to five or six, a strong Super-ego but little moral sense. Through the Oedipus Complex, however, the Super-ego becomes involved in questions of a moral nature. These come at first in the form of danger, not as matters of right or wrong. If the child uses 'right' and 'wrong' as terms to describe this or that action he is using them in a social sense rather than a moral one. That is to say, he is repeating a judgement he has learned from his parents or others and 'right' simply means to him what he knows his parents approve and call by that word. His repetition of the word, even apparently correctly, does not mean he understands its full implications or that he is capable at this stage of doing so. In fact he has not yet acquired the mental structure to make the judgement. All that the child knows is that certain kinds of actions win the approval of his parents and stimulate their love for him, and that others provoke their disapproval and even their actual hostility in the form of a physical assault upon his person – they call it punishment, but to him it is aggression. Discretion and the need to preserve their love usually teach him to choose what they call right and avoid what they call wrong.

We have seen how the Oedipus Complex develops in the boy's love for his mother and rivalry with the father and how, to avoid the destruction his intense longing for the mother threatens to bring, he introjects the father-image to enable him to control his libidinal attachment to his mother and finally to renounce her as a sexual object. By means of this introjection his passionate sensuous love becomes tender affection, 'aim-inhibited love', love from which sensuous fulfilment is repressed. The father-image becomes a part of the Ego, but a special part of it. Earlier stages of the Super-ego are embodied in it. The Super-ego has thus undergone two changes from its earlier forms. In the first place it has become, as it were, personalised. It is the psychical representative of the supreme authority which the boy ascribed to the father and which is now the self expressing itself authoritatively. The boy has achieved this stage by accepting the ruling of the father and by a psychological identification with him, so that henceforth the voice of the Super-ego is his own voice, with accepted authority over every other impulse. It is perceived neither as coming from an external source nor as being subject to qualifications of preference or expediency. It thus takes on the character of an unconditional obligation, the 'ought' of morality. At the same time, and closely bound up with this development, the behests of the Super-ego become concerned with problems of conduct that fall into the class we call moral because they involve our relations with other people. The Oedipus Complex raised in the boy the intense wishes to murder his father and to marry his mother which conflicted with the fear of his father's revenge on him. The Super-ego therefore was created to deal with these two primal crimes, parricide and incest. Prohibitions against these are the nucleus of all our moral systems. The ban against them is inherent in our nature as it is shaped in the course of development, just as the desire to commit them is one of the strongest elements in us, repressed after infancy into the unconscious. It is an interesting study to work out how this influences our conceptions of the relative gravity of various sins or crimes. In many minds 'sin' is still almost synonymous with 'illicit sexual indulgence'.

To the Super-ego formed in this way are added the standards subsequently acquired from various sources – school, home, Church, society, and so on – and the authority of the Super-ego is given to them in the degree to which they are incorporated in the self. Once we accept them they take on the character of ought. We do not, of course, adopt every standard we hear of. There is always some measure of identification as the means by which we take on new standards. It is an emotional process rather than an intellectual one. But I shall come back to that later.

It is clear, then, that we acquire our so-called 'moral sense' in the course of normal development, even though it is not a special organ with which we are endowed. It is clear also that we acquire from our social environment the moral standards which are enforced by our Super-ego, except for the two primal standards forbidding incest and parricide. It is also clear that the function of the Super-ego in exacting moral standards is only one of its activities derived from the deeper function of safeguarding the Ego from psychological danger. It enforces moral standards because these become psychologically identified with control of the primal urges, and therefore indulgence in any of the impulses against which the standards are directed is equivalent to indulgence in the primal urges and that means exposing the Ego to destruction at the hands of the primal father. There is, therefore, nothing in the working of the Super-ego to guarantee any infallible accuracy in its judgements. It just likes what it likes and detests what it detests and an action, or impulse to action, is 'right' or 'wrong' because it is approved or abhorred by the Super-ego. And because we are all susceptible to abnormalities of development the Super-ego may be abnormal in its judgements. Hence I said that a strong conscience is not at all a sure sign of moral goodness.

The phrase 'moral goodness' implies that we can draw a distinction between conscience and morality. Terminology can mislead us here so we need to clarify our meanings. There are three factors involved when we make a judgement about right and wrong. There is, first, the content of the judgement – 'it is wrong to murder'; there is, secondly, the feeling of obligation not to commit murder; and thirdly there are the arguments from reason which we can put forward to justify the judgement. The first two factors are subjective and the usual procedure is to call them conscience – 'My conscience forbids me to steal'. The third factor is objective, for it implies reference to some standards of goodness which are independent of the individual's opinions, either standards to which he is expected to conform – 'That's not cricket', 'not fair', 'not Christian', and so forth – or standards for which he is searching by a factual study of the results of different kinds of action – sometimes called 'positivist ethics'. The existence of such external standards implies that we do not regard the subjective standards as intrinsically ultimate measures of right and wrong. Conscience can give wrong judgements according to them. The search for these objective standards is the work of the Ego under the stimulus of the Super-ego, but temporarily freed from the compulsive 'ought'. Once a decision about standards has been reached the suspension of the 'ought' ceases and the new standard is subjectively adopted as part of conscience. We could well use 'moral judgement' to refer to these standards reached through reasoning over observed facts, and 'conscience' for spontaneous intuitive behests. The sense of obligation to act by them is the moral element. In the case of the subjective intuitions it is already attached when the behest appears in consciousness. In the other case it becomes attached when the Ego accepts, either implicitly or explicitly, the objective standard presented to it or makes its own moral judgement. Morality thus covers both the subjective and objective factors and is wider than conscience. It should be noted that the objective standards are susceptible to error, so the sense of 'ought' attaching to them is no more a guarantee of their rightness than it is of the subjective behests of conscience.

In revealing how conscience develops and functions, psychoanalysis thus deprives us of any infallible guide to what is right and wrong, and this without taking account of the abnormalities which may occur in the development of the Super-ego and distort its functioning. One particular aspect of the working of the Super-ego confirms this. In previous chapters we have seen how the mechanism of displacement obtains substitute gratification for repressed wishes. The Super-ego is of course involved in this. In the unconscious levels of the mind it scrutinizes the impulses from the Id and resists those it judges to be dangerous – in the sense explained above. The repressed impulse changes its form and seeks expression in a new way. This new way may penetrate into consciousness but is still resisted, though not repressed by the Super-ego. Let me give a hypothetical illustration. A common infantile impulse persisting in the unconscious is to devour father or mother or brothers and sisters. This repressed impulse is allowed into the conscious only in the form of the idea of eating meat. The Super-ego detects the association and opposes the old impulse in its new form and, as a reaction against the repressed impulse, compels the individual to become a vegetarian. I hasten to add that there are quite reasonable grounds to support a preference for vegetarianism. Nevertheless such a complex of motives does support some vegetarians. In this case the secondary taboo – not to eat meat – may perhaps be called an aesthetic judgement, though some people make it almost a moral one. But in a similar way the repression of a wish to murder the father may appear in consciousness as a resistance to killing of any kind and so produce a conscientious objector who treats his belief as a moral principle, which indeed it is to him. If, however, analysis were to resolve his unconscious impulse to parricide, we could well expect the conscientious scruples to disappear, since they would no longer be serving their primary purpose of safeguarding the Ego against the forbidden wish. Again, of course, this is not the sole or necessary reason why people become conscientious objectors. Undoubtedly, however, in many cases what we believe we hold as moral principles are really reactions against displaced unconscious impulses. In such cases the severity of the reaction against them is more appropriate to the original unconscious wish than to the form allowed into consciousness. The strength with which we hold a particular moral conviction therefore is not a sound indication of its importance, nor is it a guarantee that in other matters we are governed by high moral principles. This was one of the charges made by Jesus against the Pharisees. They strained at a gnat, but would easily swallow a camel. In making this criticism, he was judging the worth of their conduct by standards other than theirs. He was not accusing them of conscious hypocrisy, but was attacking their moral judgement. They were indignant because he was criticizing beliefs they held to be very important. They confused their own zeal with right judgement and were not prepared to learn from the new teaching. Fanaticism of this nature is almost always the certain sign of a displacement, or of a reaction formation against strong repressed wishes. Moral zeal against sin is apt to be a defence on the part of the self against unconscious wishes of the type attacked. In the eyes of Jesus, a strong conscientious conviction of doing right is not a justification for wrong conduct. He taught that we must be ready to hold our beliefs to the death, but we are equally bound to see that they are right beliefs. Christian morals, therefore, are not derived from a strong Super-ego.

We do not avoid this danger by the expedient of ascribing our moral beliefs to God, borrowing His authority to support them. The Pharisees did that. Their God was simply a projection of the unconscious father-image, the core of the Super-ego, and because they gave supremacy to it, their God was not the real God with Whom Jesus was concerned and Who could be seen in the lilies of the field, in the farmer sowing his crop, or a father welcoming home a long-lost son, that is, a God discoverable by the Ego. Theirs was an authoritarian God, the projected infantile image of the father, unmodified by knowledge of the real father. Any authoritarian system of morals, whether it ascribe authority to God or the Church, if it is accepted uncritically, depends on the Super-ego. It does not matter whether it call itself Christian or not; it is opposed to the Christian principle of using eyes and ears to learn for oneself.

It is not the Super-ego but the Ego which should play the chief part in determining what is good, the pursuit of which constitutes the right. The Ego relies on its reality-sense and power of reasoning, by which it weighs facts and their connexions and regulates conduct accordingly. It builds up a sense of relative values which are not simply accepted on authority but are based on insight into the world of things and people. In moral matters it thinks freely about the problems of conduct and is guided by the principle expressed in 'By their fruits ye shall know them.' Of course no one can work out every problem for himself, but we must have reasonable grounds for accepting guidance from an outside source. Reflection and testing, experiment maybe, using one's intelligence to the full, is the mark of an active Ego, as it accepts or rejects this or that moral direction. It does not matter whether it comes from the intuitive promptings of conscience or from friend, preacher, Bible, what you will – all must be subjected to scrutiny.

Because a dominating Super-ego is a hindrance in the pursuit of the good, it does not follow that a weak Super-ego or none at all is desirable. A purely positive system of morals that has no feeling of obligation, of an unconditional 'ought', and is simply a statement of the consequences of action, is impossible in a mind that has developed to maturity. A Super-ego is part of our normal make-up and that means that it is normal for us to feel a sense of moral duty. What is crucial is the system of morals it prescribes. A weak Super-ego would mean that the Id is not brought under control. Control of the Id and its impulses is the very condition of that cultural and social development, both in society and the individual, which we call civilization, as we have seen in an earlier chapter. Again, an apparently weak Super-ego, manifesting itself in indifference to moral obligations, can easily be the result of an unresolved Oedipus Complex and mean that an infantile outlook persists into adulthood. Normal development does not evade the Oedipus Complex. It grows through it. The only way to grow through it is that we have described – by introjecting the father and forming a Super-ego. If, however, we get 'fixated' in the Oedipus Complex, or at any earlier stage, we may not develop a Super-ego in any strength. The 'freethinker' in morals is not free at all. He is bound by severe repressions and is an undeveloped infant defying the psychological father-image with whom he dare not come to terms.

A truly free Ego is the result of balanced relations in the triangle of the Id, the Super-ego and Ego. This means that there is no severe persisting conflict between Id and Super-ego, and that the Ego is strong relative to both. To put it another way, it means that the Ego is able to persuade both to accept the guidance of the reality principle. The Id will forgo its primitive desires and accept what the Ego tells it is possible, and the Super-ego will not try to compel the Ego to conform to patterns laid down in infancy but will adapt its standards to what proves good in reality. In return the Ego will be able to serve the Id more vigorously and will be more courageous in the pursuit of the good in loyalty to the Super-ego. The Ego is their agent in all that concerns contact with the real world, in which alone can the Id find permanent satisfactions and the quality of life be tested. In the last resort it is the Ego and not the Super-ego which can test out moral standards. It needs, on the one hand, to be freed from the savagery of an infantile Super-ego, and, on the other, it needs the help of the Super-ego in handling the Id wisely. We shall return to that in the next chapter.

Both Ego and Super-ego must grow up and forsake infantile fixations. The ease with which this will be achieved depends a great deal on the development of the personality in the first five years of life. If we are to bring up children to be morally strong we shall not concentrate on teaching them codes of conduct but on assisting their emotional development so that they are not subjected to too severe libidinal stresses, leading later to conflicts with savage Super-egos. We shall try to give them Egos able to face reality with curiosity and with confidence. In this way the ideals which the Super-ego will present to the Ego for fulfilment will be both attainable by the Ego and also founded on standards that grow richer with the wisdom of experience. Good conduct is not a mould to be imposed on the Ego. It is a growth from within to be nurtured.

They are lucky people who have had such an infancy. It is not too much to hope that one of the results of psychoanalysis will be to bring it to an increasing number. Meanwhile, we may ask whether there is any escape out of conflict to goodness for those who are burdened with weakened Egos and severe Super-egos. That is a question to which the next chapter will be devoted.

CHAPTER II

THE SUPER-EGO, SIN, AND ATONEMENT

THE word 'sin' is used with different meanings, largely, one suspects, because of the failure to understand the true nature of moral action and the tendency to see it as originating in a transcendent source. In its simplest use the term means conduct by an individual contrary to what his conscience or moral judgement believes to be right. This view assumes that the highest good a man can do is to act according to his conscience. It also tends to assume that 'man must needs love the highest when he sees it.' The second meaning given to 'sin' is conduct contrary to the will of God. This assumes that independently of what the individual believes there is an absolute good, which Christians call the will of God. A man's conduct is only good when he does what this prescribes. His opinions of what is right are irrelevant. His conscience may prompt him to the right action but it may also prompt him to conduct different from what the will of God prescribes. In the latter case, even though he acts according to his conscience, he is a sinner.

We ought to reserve the term 'sin' for the first meaning and call the second 'evil' or 'wrong-doing'. We are here concerned with the first, and only with the second in so far as we need to study the psychological processes by which an individual educates his conscience from its infantile promptings to approximate more closely to the absolute good, the will of God. The general conditions of this growth we have glanced at towards the end of the last chapter. In studying the ways in which sin, in the first sense, can be overcome we shall get more light on the steps by which we learn to find the absolute good and progressively overcome evil in ourselves.

In view of the fact that the Super-ego is part of our make-up and appears to hold a position of ascendancy over the Ego, it may seem strange that sin can happen at all, that the Ego can defy the Super-ego and undertake action contrary to the commands of conscience. The reason, of course, is that the Ego serves three masters and the pressure from the Id is the prime mover. The Ego is a part of the Id modified by contact with reality. The Super-ego was created by the Ego to assist it in the task of controlling and directing the Id. The Ego may find itself with an insistent demand from the Id, for which no adequate substitutes are available and the possible satisfactions in the real world strictly limited. In such a case the Ego may have to defy the Super-ego. A very hungry man will steal food if he can get it no other way. In any such circumstances the Id is liable to overwhelm the Ego and force it into action which the Super-ego condemns. The only way in which the latter can assure that its commands are fully carried out is by effecting a complete repression of the forbidden wish, so that it does not reach consciousness and the Ego is not called to act on it. If a substitute wish reaches the Ego it means the Super-ego has already compromised on it and by virtue of allowing it to consciousness is prepared to let it pass into action, even though it be with disapproval, if no approved satisfaction is available in the real world.

In these cases where the Super-ego disapproves of action taken by the Ego under the pressure of the Id, it manifests its disapproval by a condemnation of the Ego which causes the Ego to feel a sense of guilt. This is akin to a feeling of loss of love that the infant experiences when he feels his mother or father has withdrawn the love so necessary to his psychological well-being. It is a feeling of unworthiness, of insecurity, of having evoked hostility. The Ego tries to evade this condemnation, this painful sense of guilt, by bringing forward excuses such as 'I couldn't help it', 'I really meant to do good', 'If I hadn't done that, something worse would have happened', 'Everybody does it', and so on, all of which are attempts to change the standards of the Super-ego in respect of the particular action. Sometimes they succeed and the sense of guilt disappears. This does not necessarily mean a lowering of moral standards, though it often is, for it is desirable that the Super-ego should be educable to new standards. A displaced sense of guilt, one that we have seen is sometimes out of all reasonable proportion to the importance of the act, does not as a rule respond to such reasoning because it does not touch the unconscious crime against which the condemnation is directed. During the late war I had to try to help a woman who came from the north of England in order to confess that she had caused the war. She was in great mental distress over it. When she was confirmed twenty years earlier she had not made her confession beforehand. This had angered God, who had sent the war to punish her. Needless to say, she was not responsive to reasoning. In exceptional cases of a clearly neurotic character the Ego may feel a sense of guilt which cannot be attached to any particular action, guilt which arises from a wish that remains repressed and whose displacements are too far removed from it for the guilt to follow them.

In this connexion, it should be remembered that the unconscious works by the primary system of thinking, in which fantasies and wishes are realities. The unconscious mind does not draw a distinction between the thought and the deed as does the Ego, working by the reality principle. The Super-ego working in the unconscious levels of the mind is governed by the same primary system and treats unconscious fantasies as realities. This is why there can be a sense of guilt when no act has apparently been done which justifies the condemnation thus expressed by the Super-ego. It is concerned with psychological reality, not with objective occurrences. An interesting illustration of the way this feeling of guilt can work is shown in the behaviour of certain *very* offenders guilty of various crimes. These are *com-* *been* because they have committed the crimes. The *unscious* mitted the crimes because they felt guilty. *a way of* tormented by a feeling of guilt rising *mit actual* conflicts and not attachable to any con*nus tries to* escape from this intolerable situa*ove the guilt.* crimes to which the guilt can f*ering, helps to* bring about a situation it can *k* can find means of expia*t* Acceptance of loss, of restore harmony between the Ego and the Super-ego. Analysts find that many hysterical patients are really happy in their sufferings. They are the displacements of their unconscious fantasies but they are also the expiation of the guilt attaching to them.

Here too is to be found the explanation of Original Sin. Theologians differ about what this term really means. It denotes something in human nature that is more than a disposition to sin. It is mythologically described as an inheritance from the sin of Adam, a taint which is in every man but is not the consequence of his own action, so that from the first moment of his life he is alienated from God. It is not our concern to discuss the theological conception here, but psychoanalysis has thrown considerable light on what underlies the conception. The sense of sin comes, we have seen, from the personalisation of the Super-ego at the resolution of the Oedipus Complex, by which the wish to destroy the father and possess the mother are mastered in the developing infant. If these wishes had not existed there would have been no need to form the Super-ego and so develop a moral conscience. Thus the precondition of getting a knowledge of good and evil at all is that we have sinned psychologically. A sense of guilt is inherent in our make up. The original sin is the complex of wishes in the Oedipus Complex which we develop before we have a moral sense, but which remain, in varying degrees of fixation, after we have developed that moral sense in dealing with them as dangerous wishes. It is therefore due to something which happens in the life-time of the individual, the development of the whole complex structure of relations and so of the human mind – by which we know sin – is due to the long prehistory of man. Thus the ins are both right and wrong. The conception of a of guilt innocence before the 'Fall' is a fantasy about and a fancy before the Super-ego imposed feelings are rapi. When the Oedipus Complex is resolved memorie reby developed the memories of infancy d henceforth function as unconscious an carries about with him the unconscious memory of a time when he was free from the sense of guilt. Since he now has a moral sense this is naturally interpreted by him as a time of sinlessness, of innocence. In reality the desires now judged sinful were present in full force, but the Super-ego was not passing judgement on them. The 'Fall' is not something subsequent to the acquisition of a moral sense, it is, as it were, the precondition of it. The grown man thus inherits from his infancy a sense of having sinned, as well as a tendency to sin through the pressure of the Id driving the Ego away from the guidance of the Super-ego.

But the Ego's service of the Super-ego is not simply the passive one of receiving orders to do this and refrain from that, it actively aspires to become what the Super-ego wants it to be. In the Super-ego is set the Ego-ideal, the ideal self, to which the Ego tries to conform. In the measure that it succeeds it experiences a sense of well-being, of happiness and confidence that can rise in extreme cases to the ecstasy of bliss. It is the analogue of the infant who is assured of being fully loved by the mother. When the Ego behaves in a way that falls short of the Ego-ideal and so draws on itself the condemnation of the Super-ego, the resultant feeling is one of unworthiness, of hopelessness, of guilt, that is very painful and from which the Ego tries to escape.

The quest for the restoration of harmonious relations between the Ego and the Super-ego is one of the central themes of the Christian religion, where it appears as the struggle to overthrow sin and attain pureness of life. In its fullest form it is the doctrine of the Atonement through Christ. The light that psychoanalysis throws on the structure and functioning of the human mind can help us here to distinguish what is healthy from what is abnormal.

The problem is twofold. First, there is the general problem of making the individual's life conform to the ideal standard which is laid down by Christ and is independent of his own beliefs. The interpretations of that standard vary but we have seen in earlier chapters various ways in which we can get some guidance from psychoanalysis to help us interpret Christ's life and teaching. The second problem is the personal one of trying to live according to the standards of conscience and achieve sinlessness in the narrower sense. The two problems are not in practice separated, but the emphasis varies according to the type of character produced by the interrelations of Ego, Id and Super-ego in different people.

There is a large section of Christian teaching which believes that the ideal Christian life is attained by having a dominating Super-ego strong enough to enforce all its demands on the Ego and to suppress the Id. This type of Christianity concentrates in its moral teaching on developing a sense of sin, which means, psychologically, sharpening the subservience of the Ego to the Super-ego at the expense of the Id. The Ego is made to feel its unworthiness, its failure to live up to its ideal, and is discouraged in every way from rebelling against the Super-ego. As an acknowledgement of its guilt all sorts of penances are encouraged – rigid discipline of life, fasting, acts of duty. Duty is the keynote of this moral system. The result of this training frequently is to develop a sort of vicious circle. By cultivating a sense of sin and strengthening the dominance of the Super-ego the Ego is made to feel its guilt and unworthiness more intensely. But the more guilty the Ego feels the more strongly the Super-ego attacks it, thereby further increasing the feeling of guilt. So the circle goes on until the Ego is almost paralysed from undertaking novel action. The only brake on the process is obtained through penances and mortification, even to the extent of self-inflicted pain. By accepting these the Ego is able to regain some of its self-esteem, for they are the token of its obedience to the Super-ego. Further, since in this type of character there is usually a strong masochistic (enjoyment of suffering) tendency in the unconscious, the Id gets satisfaction from the suffering and its pressure on the Ego is reduced in other directions. The masochistic tendency in the Id is matched by the aggressive sadistic component of the Super-ego, so that this severe self-discipline produces a considerable libidinal pleasure and is not simply a moral achievement. The more the dominance of the Super-ego grows the more it reverts to its non-moral pre-Oedipus character. Fasting and mortification and self-denial are often regarded as the sign of holiness. Psychoanalysis shows that they readily become perversions of the Id and a crippling of the Ego that renders the personality unable to cope with the problems of life. It forces a retreat from life to a hermitage or convent. It is not a religion for this world. It is an escape from this world, its interests and its works, into the other world.

I have spoken of it as strengthening the Super-ego. In practice we find stress is laid on the wrath of God against sin. The righteousness of God, it is asserted, cannot compromise with sin and must destroy the sinner unless he repents and puts aside his sins. This opens the way to the wider conception of sin as something more than defying one's own conscience – acting contrary to the will of God. But it also means that the Super-ego is projected on to God. This is easy. The Super-ego is the introjection of the father-image and God is the ultimate father-substitute. The effect can be psychologically disastrous where the Super-ego is already dominant. By the projection it is put out of reach of all questioning and becomes unapproachable by reason. God speaks, it is our duty to obey.

By projecting the Super-ego on to God, the standards are not made objective in fact, but only in appearance. They are put out of reach of the Ego, which is the organ of objectivity. Further, the Super-ego then comes between the Ego and the real God, for the projection masks Him. Into this God of the projected Super-ego can flow the aggressive impulses of the Id, as they did in the infantile non-moral Super-ego. This explains why in the name of God there can be cruel persecution, burning of heretics, witch-hunting and all the other fanaticisms which characterized the Inquisition and similar movements.

The Super-ego is the primal-father image come back in a new form. With the return of the primal father comes also the condemnation of the primal sins, the wishes to possess the mother and destroy the father. The infant only knows sexual longings inside the family but the condemnation of these wishes widens to include all sex and all rebellion against authority. Sex comes to be regarded as unclean, and to call a woman a sinner conveys almost only one meaning. To be a rebel against authority – a radical, a communist, a heretic – is thought to challenge the whole structure of Christianity, except by those who see a warfare between Church and State and think of the State as the enemy of God. Just as the infant feared destruction for his infantile fantasies, so the sinner can only expect to be totally destroyed by such a God. He will be punished, cast into a hell of torment in which there is only suffering, no pleasure.

Let me remind the reader that we are here considering a type of religion which is a perversion of Christianity, but which is unfortunately common enough. It is necessary to remember this, because a way of escape opens up to those who have been caught in this vicious circle, the way of atonement with God through Jesus Christ. This leads them back to Christianity, or a truncated form of it. But because it presents the issues involved in colourful and melodramatic terms it tends to attract attention more readily than the truer and richer forms of atonement and the latter may be overlooked, with the result that the perverted form comes to be regarded as the essential way to achieve the Christian life. Nevertheless, since it is sometimes easier to understand the normal through the study of the abnormal, let us continue the analysis of this type of religion.

The experience, or experiences, comprised under the term 'atonement', are thoroughly testified in experience by countless people, but there is no commonly accepted explanation of it. This might well have been expected in view of the possibility of different psychological attitudes in the approach to Christianity. On the whole, official teaching has tended to support the Super-ego type. This also is to be expected, since people who have to exercise authority tend to lean to the authoritarian point of view. All interpretations of the Atonement agree on certain basic principles, namely, that man fails to do the will of God and so is estranged from God, but that he can find reconciliation with Him through the mediation of Christ. If a man 'accepts Christ', he finds himself in what is variously called a state of 'grace', of 'salvation', of 'peace with

God', of 'forgiveness'. Let us try to disentangle the mental processes involved in this.

The Super-ego type of religion emphasizes the wrath of God and man's guilt and it strives to deepen the sense of having sinned so that to escape destruction man will seek the remedies God in His mercy has provided. The sins of man which it condemns are basically indulgence in sex and defiance of the primal father. In consciousness they will not appear as crudely as this, but in derivative form; nevertheless, adultery and disobedience will tend to rank high in the list. The primal father-God is outraged by man's sin and inevitably will destroy him. The primal father of the horde exacted complete sexual abstinence and obedience from those sons who stayed with him. He destroyed those who failed in these. So the primal father-God asks chastity and obedience. Paradoxically man can only escape the wrath of God by death, which satisfies the primal father and protects him from any challenge to his authority. Man not only inherits original sin as part of his nature but also in fact becomes a sinner and thus is unable to make the offering of perfect obedience which is what the primal father-God wants. Jesus Christ, the Son of God, came to live on earth a life of sinlessness and obedience. He was 'the lamb without blemish' – the ideal son of the primal father – the only one not deserving to be destroyed. He chose, however, out of his love, to identify himself with his human brethren and voluntarily accepted their inevitable fate – death. At last the perfect sacrifice was made in full to the God outraged by man's sin. Other men can appropriate the benefits of this sacrifice of Christ by identifying themselves with him, by making him their Lord, by striving to unite themselves to him in prayer and sacrament, by showing a like spirit of acceptance of suffering and sacrifice in their lives, by absolute obedience to his commands. This interpretation of the Atonement throws the emphasis on sin, suffering and death. Death in the unconscious, which is infantile in its nature, is the equivalent of castration, feared by the infant son at the hands of his jealous father. A few diehards teach a point of view that seems to be almost completely objective, in that the death of Christ has once and for all paid the full penalty for the sins of all mankind irrespective of what they believe about it. But the key to atonement is the identification with Christ.

This process of identification is so important in the development of the personality, and particularly in this connexion, that we need to consider it at this point in more detail. This will enable us to understand how Christ can transform us and what it means psychologically to 'accept Christ'. Identification is the most important psychological mechanism in effecting changes in the Ego, particularly those which concern emotional development and character. A free Ego, working by the reality principle, can acquire increased knowledge of the world and learn how to act more effectively on its environment of men and things. This is, as it were, a sharpening of the mind as an instrument. It does not necessarily imply a development in the basic character of the particular person, unless of course, some mastery of psychoanalysis is part of the knowledge and it is applied relentlessly in self-analysis. Psychoanalytic treatment can do a great deal to set free many types of people who are suffering from unconscious conflicts and abnormalities of development and can be a source of strength to those who are relatively normal, but a course of treatment is available only to a very few people and is akin in the mental sphere to a surgical operation for bodily ailments.

Changes in character, as distinct from the acquisition of theoretical and practical knowledge, usually come by another means. Knowledge *per se* is not virtue. Normal and abnormal people alike use identification as a means of adaptation to other people. The process operates from birth. By means of it an individual projects himself into the world and takes the world into himself and in so doing adopts the character of something that had been outside, independent of himself. The outstanding case of such identification that we have examined in preceding pages is that of the son with the father, in the throes of the Oedipus Complex, enabling him to introject the father-image and modify his Ego by forming a Super-ego. I think it was Freud (I cannot trace the reference) who said that the analysis of a woman enables an analyst to discover the characters of the men she has loved because she has identified herself with them, and each successive identification has left its mark in the modifications of the Ego it has produced.

The conditions which favour identification are of three chief kinds. First it is brought about if there is a libidinal attachment to the object. This may be of a positive or negative character, love or hate. We grow like the people we love or hate. This is more than mere imitation. In the case of love the assimilation of character may in part be conscious, but it is certainly not so with hate. Because of our emotional interest in others we project ourselves into them, as it were, and thus live out our lives in them and they become part of us. The second kind of condition predisposing to identification is similarity of circumstances. This may cover a wide range of resemblances, from the most superficial to the most profound. The study of dreams shows what trivial connexions can be used as a basis of identification, and ordinary life shows how strong are the bonds between people whose lives have run a parallel course. Take such a simple illustration as *esprit de corps*. It is based almost entirely on identification. The third mode of identification is closely allied to this. It occurs between those who have adopted a common Ego-ideal. It is manifested a great deal in the behaviour of groups, whether transient mobs or more permanent group organizations. Freud has made a penetrating study of it in his *Group Psychology and the Analysis of the Ego*. An army, through admiration of its commander, becomes knit together in bonds of identity. So does the Church, says Freud, through accepting Jesus as the common Ego-ideal. Freud goes on to analyse some of the consequences of this attitude, but unfortunately he assumes that Christianity is always of the type which we have been examining in the preceding paragraphs, the type we have called Super-ego religion.

To return to the Atonement in this type of Christianity. It is achieved through identification with Christ, whose life was one of perfect obedience to God the Father, whose Son he was. Identification with him is encouraged first by the way he identified himself with man and secondly by the fact that he suffered the very penalities that we, in our unconscious, fear as the just punishment of our unconscious crimes, whose derivatives we openly confess. He is our representative, the perfect man accepting that punishment on our behalf, though as an individual he did not merit it. Through that acceptance, he finished his life in unbroken obedience. He is perfectly at one with the Father. By identifying ourselves with him we first of all reap the benefit of his sinlessness because we inherit from him the Father's forgiveness of our sins, and, secondly, we put on his character. He lives in us and we in him and our character becomes modelled on his. We gain the strength we need to cease from sin – that is, from disobedience and lust. The vicious circle is broken, the burden of guilt drops away from our shoulders. The scarlet of our sins is washed away and we become as white as snow. We are 'washed in the blood of the Lamb'. We escape, therefore, from the condemnation of the Super-ego, inwardly shown in the sense of guilt and outwardly in the fear of God, and we know an unspeakable sense of joy, the joy that always comes when the Ego approximates to the Ego-ideal.

There are many variants of this experience of Atonement, which is undoubtedly achieved by many people. The characteristics of it are the approach through a sense of sin and guilt, the emphasis on suffering and death, on obedience and sexual purity, in ourselves and in Christ, and on the joy of being set free from our sins. It is undoubtedly a real experience of freedom and release and a source of strength. It is a grave error to dismiss it as a fantasy. It is a way of escape from the vicious circle of self-condemnation and its paralysis back to reality and freedom of action. But it is subject to the limitations of the Super-ego type of religion. Whilst it brings freedom from the sense of guilt and power to do the will of God, that will is interpreted according to the limitations of the Super-ego outlook as the avoidance of sin and the need to accept suffering and hardship as a means of satisfying God's wrath. It frequently also produces a somewhat paradoxical situation. The 'saved' sinner goes on calling himself a miserable sinner (he has to do this to keep the Atonement psychologically effective, for unless

he continues to feel guilty he does not feel the need of reconciliation with God), but at the same time he is apt to think of
himself as one of the elect of God. He dare not claim for himself any share in his own salvation, but must ascribe it to the
mercy of God through Christ. To claim any part in it would
be to challenge the absolute authority of God, to revive one of
the primal sins. Since therefore it was all the work of God, the
saved must be specially chosen by God. This in turn leads
sometimes to spiritual pride and unctuousness, in which the
apparent confession of sin is an empty formula used as a cloak
to justify the open condemnation of the sins of other less for-
tunate people. It is true that the 'saved' are frequently filled
with a great desire to 'preach the gospel' to other people, but
the gospel they preach is the narrow one of guilt and salvation
they themselves have experienced.

Viewed psychologically, and religiously, those more extreme cases have only achieved a partial release. They have got
release from a particular conflict, but have failed to get the full
freedom which can only come from a thorough readjustment
of the balance of power between the Ego, Id, and Super-ego.
Their identification with Christ has only been a partial one.
They have not understood him fully, but have selected from
his life those elements which fortified their Super-ego outlook, or they have even read into him their own preoccupation
with the wrath of God and the virtues of suffering and obedience. Nevertheless, there is always a real gain, because in the
identification with Christ they cannot entirely limit him to the
partial understanding with which they began, and they put
on something of his real character. They even become in some
degree conformed to him. They may even grow beyond their
early bondage to the Super-ego and win to the full freedom of
the Christian life of love.

This usually comes from reading the Bible. They go to it to
read the story of Christ. The picture of him that is given there
is considerably different from the one they read into him from
their guilt-laden minds, and through constant reading some of
the characteristics of the true Christ begin to emerge more
clearly and become incorporated in them through the identi-

fication. In other words, they more truly 'find Christ' objectively and he becomes more to them than the projection of their own image. In the measure that they find Christ objectively they gain a real freedom and make real growth and do not simply get release of a psychological tension expressed in the sense of guilt. There is a difference between being filled with Christ and obsessed with him. The Christ-filled character has really grown to be like him, because through identification the Ego has taken on the character of the real Christ and has gained a new outlook, freed from the domination of the fanatical Super-ego, which manifests itself by a frenzied insistence on the destructive, vengeful wrath of God. When Christ is an obsession with us, we may spend our time talking about him and his holiness and we may be trying to serve him. Nevertheless, the identification has really been in the reverse direction – we have identified Christ with ourselves and given him our character, put ourselves in his place. This projection of ourselves and our values on to him then blinds us to any understanding of him as he really is, and so the real Christ cannot grow in us. Our chief preoccupation continues to be sin, not love. As he himself said, not the profession, but the fruit is the test. 'Not everyone that saith unto me, Lord, Lord, shall enter into the kingdom of Heaven, but he that doeth the will of My Father which is in Heaven.' No matter how devotedly we may serve a false Christ, it does not make him the real Christ, nor ourselves true Christians.

Two of the chief marks of a Christian are freedom and love. Psychoanalysis shows that they cannot be produced by what I have called Super-ego religion, with its emphasis on sin, guilt and punishment – its castration complex. It is a hindrance to try to be a Christian in that way, for while some do win through to a genuine knowledge of Christ and all that that means, most who pursue this road get caught in the vicious circle of the savage Super-ego lashing a guilty punishment-seeking Ego, and their spiritual growth is paralysed. The true atonement lies by another road.

CHAPTER 12

THE EGO AND THE LOVE OF JESUS

A DISPASSIONATE reading of the Gospels forces us to believe that Jesus was not primarily interested in sin. It is true that he is recorded as using phrases such as 'Thy sins be forgiven thee', but in the test case presented to him of the woman taken in adultery, he did not condemn the woman, but sent accusers and accused away to think again. His strongest condemnation was against hypocrites and those who misled or thwarted the aspirations of the young and the spiritually hungry – that is, against people who thought themselves sinless. In this he differs from the attitude we were considering in the last chapter. A further point we note about him is that he seems to believe quite confidently that his followers can and will become like him. 'I have called you friends,' 'Greater things than these shall ye do,' 'Be ye perfect,' and so he claims for man more than most Christians are prepared to claim. The difference between him and the traditional Christian is not merely that the latter is a sinner and knows himself to be one, whereas Christ knew himself to be without sin. The difference is much more a matter of emphasis on values, a question of what is of primary importance. The Super-ego type of Christian may use Christ for relief from his sense of guilt, but he does not understand Christ. I would almost be inclined to say that he understands the Christ of theology, but not the Christ of the Gospels. But that does less than justice to a great many theologians.

There is another type of religion which is more akin to that of Christ and which opens up the way to him for the ordinary man. It is what I call Ego-religion, a vastly different thing, of course, from self-worship, and having nothing to do with egotism, the pursuit of self-interest. Ego-religion springs not from the strictures of the Super-ego but from the Ego's grasp of the nature of the real world and its attempts to deal with that world in such a way as to give most effective expression to the impulses coming from the Id. Instead of leading to paralysis and a retreat from the world, it opens up the way to fuller life – the abundant life promised by Christ. It does not lay primary stress on the sense of sin; nevertheless, an atonement is part of it, is necessary too, for it requires oneness with God. But this oneness with God is not the spectacular business of 'conversion' or repentance found in the Super-ego type of religion. It requires identification with Christ like the other, but it is on the whole a steady, strong growth of the personality, taking place through many stages of development that are sometimes so gradual that they are scarcely noticeable. Nevertheless the Super-ego enters into Ego-religion. It is a guide rather than a dictator.

To help us understand the nature of healthy religion, let us restate the problem of human development in its broad outlines. The growing boy has to face two major problems. He has to come to grips with the real world and he has to solve his relationships with his father. These are not separate problems. They are interrelated, and the solution of the one will help to solve the other. As the problem of facing the real world arises first, success in it is more likely to contribute to successful relations with the father than the reverse. Both problems arise out of the flow of demands from the Id, the source of all desire. These instinctive demands can only find final satisfaction upon the real world, animate and inanimate, so under their pressure the developing Ego tries to lead them to make appropriate contact with the world. The Ego sets out to explore and master the world. This is the genesis of the scientific and technical side of life. Science and its inventions are the furthest developments of this impulse and of the Ego to increase the satisfactions it can offer to the Id. In gathering knowledge about the nature of the world and skill in handling it, the Ego develops its strength. The world is not always easy to master. It is sometimes dangerous. If the infant Ego finds it too difficult or too painful, it may be forced to turn back in upon itself to fight the demands of the Id which it cannot satisfy. It sets up repressions and the Id can only get expression in fantasies. The demands from the Id that create the greatest problem are those that produce the Oedipus Complex. They ultimately force the Ego to set up the Super-ego, that is, to accept as part of its constitution the internal father – son conflict as the price of survival and continued growth. Thus the second great problem is created. To the need to get knowledge of the real world as the way to instinctual satisfaction is added a condition through which the Ego must of its own nature work from then on. It must conform to the standards or ideals determined by the Super-ego. This is the moral factor. The subsequent development of the man will reveal as one of its aspects the attempt to combine the scientific and the moral aspects of life.

The use of the word 'scientific' in this connexion lays us open to confusion of thought. We may think of science as a body of ideas or knowledge about the world which we can learn and use. This is a common and no doubt justifiable use of the term. But science is something more profound than that; it is a way of thinking about the world, a way of getting to know it. Science does not try to impose preconceived notions upon the world, except as working assumptions, but tries to discover how the world works. By means of this method, scientists have accumulated a body of knowledge which is called 'science' or 'scientific', but in the stricter meaning it is possible to learn all this and yet not be truly scientific, because we have not adopted the scientific method or outlook which exalts fact over idea. It is easy to hold 'science' in a dogmatic way – that is, in a quite unscientific way in the deeper sense. Many people who are learned in the discoveries of science or in kindred intellectual studies are not as scientific as some unlearned peasant who is able to judge men and events objectively and realistically. The reality-thinking of the Ego is scientific in the deeper sense, which explains why so-called 'scientists' often fail to think realistically or scientifically on many topics.

In the fully developed personality the scientific outlook of the Ego and the moral guidance of the Super-ego must combine. Out of the combination will grow wisdom, goodness and freedom. How far they can combine successfully depends on the relative strength of the Ego and Super-ego. In the previous chapter we saw the results of an over-strong Super-ego. The truly Christian way – the way that was shown in Christ and taught by him – lies neither in the surrender to the Super-ego nor in its repudiation, but in a harmonious co-operation or synthesis from which Id, Ego and Super-ego all grow in strength, because inner conflict is reduced to a minimum.

The factors which determine the severity of the internal father-son relationship of Super-ego and Ego are too many and too intricate and varied for us even to attempt to list them here, but foremost among those which conduce to a healthy development we may put the following. First of all, a healthy emotional attachment to the mother – that is, one the boy can cope with. He must not be over-stimulated or frustrated by neglect, but treated with steady love that has his welfare at heart, and is not emotional indulgence on the part of the mother. Secondly, there must also be a good positive relationship with the father, neither too indulgent nor too severe on the father's side, nor vacillating from one to the other but steady and affectionate. Thirdly, the boy needs to be treated from birth as a person in his own right and with his own rights, due account being taken of the limitations of ability and of knowledge which his immaturity of body and mind put upon him, so that he will be encouraged to have confidence in himself and in his contacts with the world. What he is must not be sacrificed to what it is hoped he will be, or those hopes will be rendered impossible of fulfilment. Fourthly, he needs to be encouraged to handle the world of things and people and to think over his experiences as much as possible so that he develops a sense of reality and finds out how to get emotional satisfactions from the world in fresh ways when his wishes are frustrated in their primary form.

All this sounds very like a description of God the Father's attitude to man as revealed by Christ – unvarying love, consideration for his welfare and proper development, understanding of his needs and his limitations, the desire to make him free and wise. And so it is. It is the problem of man's relation with God in its embryonic form. The infant must come to terms with his human father (the representative of both parents), the growing boy must solve the relationship inside his own mind in the relations between the inter-dependent component parts of his personality, and the man must find harmony with God. It is the same problem begin-ning with the child and ending in atonement with God. It is the quest both for truth and for goodness. Separation of the two or suppression of one of them destroys both and leads to the spiritual death of man.

The importance of the childhood stage is hard to over-estimate. But here we must not overlook the great strength and persistence of the mysterious life instinct by which the creative urge surmounts obstacles and frustrations. It is the deepest instinct in man and it drives him to express his kinship with God in creation. Indeed, we may look upon it as the first way God works through man. This is perhaps getting into the realms of mystical speculation. It means, however, that the mind of the infant is not as fragile or as malleable as we some-times take him to be. His direction of growth is set from birth and it is not easily turned aside. Given a family background that is emotionally stable and reasonably matter-of-fact, one that fosters trust and confidence in him, the young child will surmount his two great tasks – finding the real world and growing through the Oedipus Complex. The growth is not easy. Reality-thinking – Ego living – means readiness to face pain for the sake of what lies beyond it. It is only in the fantasies of the wishful-thinking Id that life is easy and there is no pain or struggle or renunciation.

Even in the spiritually healthiest person the Oedipus con-flict is severe and it requires a period following its resolution to modify its sharp edges and heal its wounds, to recover as it were the inner direction of growth and move forward to the succeeding stages. This is achieved in the following way. The severity of the conflict with the actual father is reduced when the father-image is introjected into the Super-ego to help control the Id, so the Ego is able to see him more objectively and less distorted by infantile fantasies. Many instances of childish naughtiness really spring from the desire to test out the father to see if he is actually as harsh and dangerous as unconscious fantasies picture him. In this way reality and fantasy are compared. Where the repression has been light and the Super-ego therefore not severe, the Ego is not greatly hampered by fantasies and is able to use its powers freely upon the real world. The objective knowledge of the father gained in this way reacts back upon the unconscious fantasy image and the discrepancy between the fears and the actuality leads to a gradual softening of the severity of the Super-ego. An element of reasoning or reality is introduced into it. The authority of the newly established Super-ego is projected upon the actual father seen more as he is and it is modified to be more like him. This, of course, is not the only projection of it, as we shall presently see, but it is an important one and a wise father can greatly help the development of his son at this point.

The foundation of a healthy development is an even balance of tensions between Id, Ego and Super-ego. In the strong Super-ego type the Ego is paralysed from developing in some directions and is therefore debarred from bringing reality to influence the Super-ego in matters belonging to them. If the Ego has been able to develop more freely there is give and take between it and the Super-ego, and the development of both is possible without crippling restrictions in any particular aspect of experience. On the other hand, aggressive defiance of authority, tradition, convention and the like is, as a rule, not a sign of freedom. It is, as we have seen, the expression of a pre-Oedipus fixation, an inability to come to terms with the father, the acceptance of an infantile state of development. It is the sign of an immature, inadequately integrated personality.

We can illustrate the three types by the general attitude to sexual matters. The pre-Oedipus type, caught in the stage of defiance of the father and father-substitutes, is ready to challenge sexual conventions and accepted morality and to get a feeling of being advanced and daring in doing so. Such people are usually fond of talking a lot about sex because their repressions compel them to think of it as a forbidden topic. Or else their defiance frequently is the assertion of a narcissism that covers a feeling of deficiency, a castration complex. It is a reaction formation. The Super-ego type oscillates between a feeling that sex is unclean (a feeling that is implicit but sometimes explicitly avowed) and sentimentalizing about the beauty of legitimate family relationships, husband and wife, parent and child. It attempts to keep the traditional moral code of family relationships unchanged at all costs and it regards with unreasoning horror any transgression of marriage or anything which appears to challenge it. This, too, is a reaction formation. It points to strongly repressed and inadequately resolved Oedipus wishes towards the mother. If they had not been too strong in the first place for the Ego, it would not have been necessary for the Ego to create such a severe Super-ego to restrain it. As a consequence the Ego cannot take control but has to echo the battle between Id and Super-ego. The Super-ego compels the Ego to swing as far as possible from the unconscious wishes of the Id. The Id wishes to make the woman (mother) unfaithful to her husband (father) so the breaking of marriage vows is most abhorrent to the Super-ego. Finally, the Ego type of religion finds sex neither a daring topic nor something unclean, but a natural instinct to be used, enjoyed and developed in the ways that best satisfy the needs of the individual and society. What these ways will be can only be determined by individual and social experience and much reflection over it to find out what is most effective. It sees nothing sacrosanct in the moral code on sex at any given moment, just as it finds nothing daring in being interested in sex. It is therefore able to develop a sexual morality based on tested principles, not on prejudices and repressions, which can only be given an appearance of reasonableness by rationalizations. It is ready to reconsider its principles and codes at any time if sufficient cause be adduced. It is free to make real growth and not just to translate fixed prejudices into new forms.

Freedom does not mean freedom only of the Ego, though I have called this Ego-religion. It means that the Id, Ego and Super-ego are all able to gain more effective expression because they have found the right relationships with each other through the leadership of the Ego. They develop together to maturer and richer functioning because of what the Ego is able to gain by its freer contacts with the real world. The infant-father conflict passes into the Oedipus conflict and its resolution there clears the way to go on to solve the conflict in the man-God conflict which has to be resolved in religion. Viewed from the point of view of morality alone there can be no solution, for the dominant element in the final solution must be love, without which no growth at all is possible. If morality be interpreted as the rule of the Super-ego, or of God the supreme projected Super-ego, a solution is denied, for the persistence of the conflict is thereby made essential. A solution is only possible if Ego and Super-ego are in harmony and the standards set by the Super-ego be accepted not as commands, something imposed on it, but as expressing the true nature of the Ego, the goal or ideal arising out of its own character towards which it is striving to grow. In other words, goodness is not obedience but growth towards perfection, and perfection is complete self-fulfilment. As the philosophers say, God is the meaning of the world, the ultimate reality. In the last resort the Ego presents Him to the Super-ego, not the reverse, as is commonly supposed. The way of obedience is the way of death, the way of love is the way of life.

In an earlier chapter we spoke of belief in God beginning from a wish-fulfilment. We saw then that the father-image is projected on to God. If God remains this, the creation of or the substitute for the Super-ego, He remains only a wish-fulfilment and represents our bondage to our unconscious conflicts. It is this bondage that St Paul describes in his Epistle to the Romans, a bondage from which he could not get free till he found the way to freedom in Christ. It is not the Super-ego, the source of morals, of duty, that leads us to the living God. It is the Ego that does this for us. The Ego fills in the details vaguely outlined in the picture drawn by the Super-ego, and if the Super-ego plays its proper role it accepts the God given to it by the Ego, a God of creation, of history, of life and love, not a God of duty or fear, of abstract righteousness. It accepts a friendly God, not a hostile God.

Co-operation of Ego and Super-ego is essential. Goodness and wisdom must develop together. The development is twofold. The Ego inherits from the Super-ego various moral ideals. These it must examine in the light of experience until they are shown to be trustworthy and capable of adequate justification as working ideals that produce good results. Those that fail to stand up to the test must be discarded. Secondly, it is the task of the Ego to extend those moral ideals or add to them. This is the more important. It does this by the process of identification.

The growing child has many opportunities of identifying himself with other people, as we have seen. Every group he belongs to provides him with fresh objects. He identifies himself with every person he admires. Nor is he confined to his actual social environment. Books, cinema, theatre, broadcasting bring imaginary heroes to his attention and provide a rich field of choice from which to select heroes in whom to live an imaginary life and satisfy his narcissism. Every such identification means that he takes a fresh character into himself and modifies his Ego-ideal accordingly, and his Ego thereupon tries to conform itself to the new pattern and accepts the new standards as binding.

The standards belonging to the different identifications usually conflict in some degree. The *esprit de corps* he learns from his school will differ from the ruthlessness of 'Four-gun Jake' his movie hero, or again maybe from those of 'gentle Jesus meek and mild', of the Sunday-school teacher. How is he to select? Sometimes some of the identifications are quickly rejected and the dominating ones fused into a composite pattern. Sometimes single attributes survive from the diverse heroes. Sometimes the Ego fails to achieve a complete integration and maintains various conflicting identifications in a relatively dissociated or unintegrated state, so that he is a different person with different standards according to circumstances. At work he accepts one code of behaviour, on Sundays another, in mixed company he is polite and clean-minded, at a stag party the life and soul of the gathering with his questionable stories and vulgar quips. He is many persons in one person.

Identification supplies the material by which the Ego and

the Super-ego grow, but it requires the correcting influence of reflective judgement to assess the value of each new thing learned by identification. Without it the personality is liable to drift from one love to another without any certainty of making real progress and frequently becomes the victim of emotional instability or of external circumstances. Real growth comes through discipleship, the method adopted by Jesus with his chosen band of followers, but discipleship can take many forms. Discipleship implies the use of both identification and reflective judgement. It begins with some form of hero-worship leading to an identification. The period of identification is one of almost uncritical absorption, of living in and through the other person, striving to see, understand, think, feel as he does, and of accepting his teaching. It is a period of growth and enrichment. It needs to be followed by a period, as it were, of digestion, in which the Ego emerges from the identification and takes stock, becoming independent of the hero. This involves critical examination of what has been learnt, appraisal in the light of knowledge and wisdom gained from other sources. In this way the Ego truly and consciously appropriates what has been gained through identification and discriminates between what is essential and what is incidental. The gain then ceases to depend on the continuance of the emotional tie. It also enables the Ego to re-appraise the leader from a new level of understanding and, if the hero justifies it, to make a further identification with fresh gains. The outcome of such discipleship is independence, not the blind acceptance of the leader and his thought. Some measure of such independent judgement seems to be shown in the story told by St John. When some of the followers of Jesus left him, he asked the Twelve, 'Would ye also go away?' Simon Peter answered him, 'Lord, to whom shall we go? Thou hast the words of eternal life.'

This independence seems to be what Jesus expected of his disciples. He asked them to follow him, to identify themselves with him, but he imposed no authority over them and gave them no clearcut system of rules and beliefs for them to accept. He made no attempt to persuade the rich young ruler, who was so close to the Kingdom of Heaven, to give up his riches and become a complete convert. He simply told him what he needed. One feels that had he made even a slight plea to the young man he would have made the necessary renunciation. In the same way, he did not try to dissuade Judas from betraying him, though he knew the betrayal would cost him his life. He expected his disciples to observe and draw the right conclusions for themselves. 'Have I been so long time with you, and dost thou not know me, Philip?' They must stand on their own feet as he stood on his and thereby was so vastly different from the Pharisees. They were not his servants, but his friends. In the same way, they were not slaves of God, but sons with all the liberty of sons.

It should now be clear what, in terms of what I have called Ego-religion, the Atonement means and how it is realized. As with the Super-ego type it means identification with Jesus, but not to escape the consequences of sin either in the form of tormenting guilt or punishment hereafter. It is identification out of love and trust rather than out of fear and guilt, identification out of life and achievement, not out of suffering and death. It requires one step more than identification in Super-ego religion, the extra step of discipleship by which we become independent of the emotional tie with him and can make a critical appraisal of what we have absorbed through following him. This does not mean repudiating him. It means seeing him more clearly. Without it we are apt to see only the Jesus our unconscious has predisposed us to see and we take into ourselves a Jesus-image, not the real Jesus, and that is one of the greatest barriers against finding the real Jesus. We have to grow step by step to become like him. With each gain in understanding, our identification becomes fuller and a corresponding change takes place in ourselves. The Atonement becomes a transformation of the personality, not the release by a psychological trick of the accumulation of emotional tension in the form of guilt. It is 'repentance' in its root sense, a change of outlook, of understanding, of values, because we have taken Jesus into ourselves and made him completely ours, because we have enlarged ourselves, not put ourselves away.

Repentance that concentrates on contrition for sins and throws the emphasis on the repudiation of them is in danger of dividing the total self instead of changing it. It seeks to disown that part which produces the sins – that is, those impulses from the Id which have come into conflict with the Super-ego – because they are expressions of the Oedipus wishes or derivations of them. The Super-ego is reinforced to put a stronger ban on them and they are pushed into the unconscious. This is not a fundamental change of outlook. What is required is not imprisonment of our natural forces but release, not condemnation but transformation.

The transformation of ourselves through identification with Jesus can only bring us atonement with God if Jesus himself was at one with God. Christians believe that he was, and point to the evidence of his life portrayed in the Gospels. They point also to the lives of those who have achieved identification with Jesus and as a result have left their mark in history. But this oneness of Jesus with God raises a peculiar problem. How did Jesus resolve his own Oedipus Complex? He must have done so to be completely at one with God. God, as we have seen, is the final stronghold, the ultimate representative or sanction of our Super-ego, and in seeking unity with God we are seeking reconciliation with our Super-ego. Jesus rightly called God 'Father', but the meaning behind it is deeper than is usually realized. God is not just our Father in a way analogous to the father of a family – a biological and social relationship. God is our 'Father' in a more direct sense, since He is the ultimate form of the Super-ego which we create out of our earthly father. The Oedipus Complex is only resolved by the son obeying the father, renouncing the mother and finding mother-substitutes which do not involve him in rivalry with the father.

But that is only the beginning of the process. We have seen that it must be carried a step further. The Super-ego God which is made out of this process has to be replaced by the Ego-God discovered in the world by the reasoning, reflecting mind, so that in the final God Ego and Super-ego meet and merge. That God is not only the sanction of morality; He is also the inner truth about the world, the meaning of reality. He is the fulfilment of the Ego as well as of the Super-ego. That the God Jesus spoke about was this kind of God seems quite clear from the Gospels, but how Jesus came to the knowledge of Him is not so clear. We have no evidence by which to determine the steps. The only insight we are given is the story told in St Luke of the visit to Jerusalem when he was twelve years old. He was left behind in the city and his parents found him a couple of days later with the teachers of religion in the Temple, 'both hearing them and asking them questions', showing a reflective mind at work. The learned doctors were amazed, we are told, 'at his understanding and his answers'. One should not try to build too much on an isolated incident, but it rings exactly true to what we should expect if the analysis in the earlier pages of this book is sound. In this incident we see Jesus discovering an Ego-God, testing and reflecting over what he had learned, using his own insight to get an understanding of God and the world. Thus we see him in the period of his ministry interested in every aspect of life and drawing illustrations from a wide range of everyday things and events – the grass, the lilies, the birds, ploughing, seed-time and harvest, house-building, the traveller among the thieves, the shepherds, the housewife, the care of vines and trees, the weather. Nothing seems to have escaped his attention. He was specially discerning about the motives of people. He understood life and loved it. He emphasized that he stood for life. He did not repudiate the urge of his Id for life. But he was realistic and not a dreamer of fantasies. He recognized that the way to fullness of life requires that we must be willing to renounce immediate satisfactions, even to give up our lives if circumstances demand it. In the Agony in the Garden of Gethsemane we see him working this principle out to the final test in his own life. The proof of his rightness would be that he would rise again from the dead. So it happened. The facts proved him right.

The at-one-ness of Jesus with God therefore involves two elements. The first is the appeasement of the hostile Super-ego God, the condemner of sins, the projection of the father-image. This perhaps may be called the way of obedience. Super-ego religion clings only to that. The second element we may call the way of attainment. It is the discovery of God in the world, the source of life and the standard of all life. By pursuing right ends we find the fullest realization of our own natural selves. And the fulfilment will express itself as love. To say that God is love is to express a factual truth. It is not adequate to say God is loving. That leaves Him too much outside the world. God is realized in us in so far as we develop love. Once this truly objective God is discovered as a fact and not as an idea or a projection, the God of the Super-ego should fade away and love replace fear. 'Perfect love casteth out fear.' It was to this that Jesus attained, and because he did he was able to make those remarkable statements about himself, such as, 'He that hath seen me hath seen the Father,' 'I and the Father are one' (identified, not identical). Attainment requires independence, not blind subservience. Love implies not a cipher, but a person. Life in God sets us free so that of ourselves we pursue the course which belongs unto God. The love of God builds up our Ego life. The three major characteristics of Christ are, therefore, objectivity, independence, love.

It would be idle to pretend that this is a complete or comprehensive analysis of Jesus. To claim to understand him fully would be, in terms of what has been said, a claim to have reached his level, to have become his equal. That is the unattained ideal of every Christian. The way towards it is helped by the fact that we can learn by being disciples of Jesus. It has been said with a large measure of truth that Christianity is caught, not taught. The average person approaches Christ through identification with people who are manifesting in their lives something of the Christ character. We can understand them more easily than Jesus and their contact with us is more concrete, more vivid. We become their disciples and grow from our identification with them. Because they have grown towards the character of Jesus, we do likewise. They lead us on the way and the more the character of Jesus enters into us the easier it becomes for us to understand him, know him, and identify ourselves with him and be led on to oneness with God through him. So it is in a fellowship that we are most likely to find Christ revealed and the Communion of Saints is the body of those who have identified themselves with Christ and are becoming like him.

This process of identification with Jesus is made central in those Christian groups which treat the service of Communion as the chief act of corporate worship. In it they 'eat the body and drink the blood' of Jesus in a spiritual way, to partake of his life, to find unity with him, to repeat his sacrifice, 'that we may dwell in him and he in us.' This mode of communion with Jesus and with one another is a development of the totem feast in which the totem animal, the representative of the tribal father, was consumed by members of the tribe in ceremonial feasts, though taboo at other times. By consuming the father, the sons incorporated his strength and spirit. The cannibal eats his enemy for the same purpose. The symbolism is obvious, but the psychological motives run deeper than the superficial symbolism. Eating the father is a fantasy of the oral phase of development. Many unconscious motives are gathered together in the rite.

In Christian Communion the purpose of identification is made conscious and deliberate. Emotion, imagination, will, are all gathered together to make the identification as effective as possible. The act of worship is a drama of union that passes into reality in the true worshipper, so that he does become identified with Jesus. The crucial test is, not the intentions, but the Jesus who is sought – that is, whether it is the Jesus created by unconscious fantasies or the real Jesus, so far as the Ego is able to discover him. Piety, religious emotion, however intense – indeed, by its very intensity – can corrupt even this act of worship unless it is counterbalanced and corrected by reflective thought. Without the latter, the worship can degenerate into superstition, into primitive ritual, satisfying dark unconscious wishes, and bind the Ego in a slavery from which it is the aim of Christianity to set it free. The drama of the Communion, therefore, must be seen only as the culmination of a much wider search after Jesus, and of God through Jesus. And it must not be seen only as a giving of ourselves, to be lost in Jesus; it is receiving the life of Jesus into ourselves that we may grow in strength and in independence. Freud has quite missed the point of this act of Christian worship because he failed to apply his own principles to its interpretation.

To sum up, then, Christianity is neither a mere moral code nor a religion of ideas. It is a historic religion and must remain so in the fullest sense, that is, in the continuity of history. It cannot be sustained on an idea about history, the recollection of the past. It grows and flourishes on facts. It is a religion of here and now. It is an Ego-religion. It is not an escape from the world, it is the conquest of the world, the physical, biological, spiritual world, the world in its fullness, of which man is an integral part. That was what Jesus meant when he said, 'I came that they may have life, and have it abundantly.' That, too, is what psychoanalysis says is possible through the reality principle by which the Ego works.

CHAPTER 13

CONCLUSION

IT may be useful by way of a conclusion to review the general lines of thought we have followed and attempt an estimate of the position we have reached. We began with the knowledge that psychoanalysis lays bare the way in which the unconscious mind manifests itself in all spheres of human behaviour, including religion. We therefore set out to explore some of its manifestations in what is generally accepted as Christianity. Since we merely aimed to explore the field, we only looked at some of the main findings of psychoanalysis, without any attempt at proof, and the early chapters of this work must not be regarded as an exposition, even in outline, of the complete system of psychoanalysis. The psychoanalytic principles expounded were selected to show that psychoanalysis furnishes a standard by which we can assess normal development (normal in the sense of reaching the full unfolding or highest degree of perfection of innate potentialities, not in the sense of average). We glanced at some of the maldevelopments that frequently occur at different stages of growth. We have examined how these maldevelopments, which lead to fixations and repressions, gain unconscious expression in Christian belief and conduct, and in the previous chapter we have seen how one form of Christianity seems to be the suitable religious expression of normal, non-fixated development.

This limited aim should be borne in mind. Many readers may have felt outraged at the cursory treatment given to the various aspects of Christianity, as, for instance, in the references to prayer. This book started off from the assumption that both psychoanalysis and Christianity are valid activities of the human spirit. We have not been aiming at a complete examination of every aspect of Christianity, but making some important tests of religion by means of a standard derived from psychoanalysis as an illustration of the way in which to measure all the elements of behaviour which are associated in people's thinking with Christianity. It is essential for the sake of that truth in which Christianity believes to discover as much as we can about the way our minds work and the true nature of our motives and beliefs. Only so can we hope to distinguish the true from the false, the good from the bad. That is why we have devoted most of the time to the way the unconscious mind enters into and shapes common Christian beliefs and attitudes. The best test of the value of what has been said is whether or not it enables the reader to get deeper insights into his own mind and religious behaviour and into the lives of others, that is, whether it helps him to overcome his own repressions and unveil in some measure his unconscious mind.

We may be tempted to think of what we have been doing as a 'psychoanalysis of Christianity', on the analogy of the analysis of an individual patient. Perhaps there is some value in the analogy, but it can be a very misleading one. The individual who undergoes psychoanalysis does so to gain freedom from the hampering effects of his unconscious conflicts. By bringing his repressions into the light of consciousness, he brings them into the sphere of the Ego-judgements of his reflective understanding, to whose functioning they now become subject, whereas before they had been governed by the infantile and distorted modes of the unconscious. A successful psychoanalysis sets the individual free to continue his mental and spiritual growth. This had been halted by the fixations and repressions. The analysis does not turn him out of the clinic fully grown up, it simply removes the obstacles to growth. But we cannot say that Christianity is subject to unconscious conflicts like an individual and so a fit subject for analysis. If by Christianity we mean a body of beliefs, practices and evaluations of life, it is meaningless to speak of the psychoanalysis of Christianity in a clinical sense, though, of course, there is always a rich meaning in the psychoanalytical interpretation of Christianity. Individual Christians, and possibly groups of Christians, are subject to repressions and manifest the usual signs of an active unconscious. This means that they suffer from the distortions of judgement and the ignorance of motivation which characterize all unconscious mental activity, and that in consequence they mistake the true significance of much that they honestly believe to be Christian.

Psychoanalysis makes a double contribution to the study, and practice, of Christianity. These are related, but it is useful to keep them distinct, for the value of the first contribution is more readily acknowledged than that of the second. First, there is the way in which it reveals the psychological character of religious beliefs, thus permitting the reflective mind to assess their relative worth, and, in so far as psychoanalysis frees individual Christians from the thraldom of their unconscious motivation, it enables them to think and to act more effectively in religious matters. The second contribution which it makes comes from the knowledge it gives us of the structure and development of the human mind and the processes by which it grows to its greatest effectiveness and thereby, we may legitimately suppose, to its highest and most complete form. To reach this mature form the infantile stages must be outgrown and fixations and unconscious conflicts reduced to a minimum. If religion cannot express itself in terms of this mature phase, it must be put aside as an infantile product. We saw that, measured by this standard, certain forms of Christianity, or what is frequently called Christianity, cannot stand up to the test and should therefore be rejected. On the other hand Christ himself and some forms of Christianity – what I have called 'Ego-religion' – meet the test at every point.

In neither case does psychoanalysis have any right to pronounce upon the truth or worth of Christianity. It reveals the psychological elements which find expression in it, but the question of ultimate truth and value are outside its scope. But psychoanalysis can and must question assumptions in Christianity which deny the accuracy of the description of the mind which it gives. It is essential to distinguish clearly between these separate functions. As a science, psychoanalysis is interested in discovering the laws of the working of the mind. As a therapeutic method, it aims to undo the knots in which the mind has become tied in the course of growth and to restore a harmony of function that will enable it to grow to maturity, or, at the lowest level, at least to work efficiently in the face of its material and social environment, where every life must be lived. It is the function of Christianity to interpret and set the goals or pattern of this development, to shape the ends, the ideals of life. Psychology cannot say whether these ends are right or wrong, good or bad in the moral sense. It can only describe the psychological aspect of their pursuit and leave it to religion to decide whether the ends should be modified in the light of what psychoanalysis reveals.

It is in this way that Freud makes his most direct and determined criticism of Christianity. It is to be found in his *Civilization and Its Discontents*. Briefly, his criticism is this. The demand by Christianity that all human conduct should be motivated by love is asking the impossible. Room must be found for the expression of the aggressive instincts, for, he says, it is extremely doubtful whether these can be fully sublimated. The attempt by Christianity to suppress all the aggressive tendencies in man is bound to fail and, in failing, to produce grave ills that will destroy the civilization that has been built up. A more reasonable appreciation of the possibilities of human nature would allow a considerable measure of freedom to the aggressive instincts and would not view their activity with the anxious concern that is shown by Christianity. Christianity is psychologically impossible of fulfilment. By aiming at a lower target, as it were, we should achieve more.

This is a weighty challenge to the basic doctrine of Christianity. It cannot be lightly dismissed by easy talk of sublimating aggression in sport, in the struggle against ignorance and evil, and so on. Freud was well aware of these fields as possibilities for the sublimation of aggression when he made his statement. On the other hand, we may believe that his acquaintance with the true nature of Christianity was inadequate and that he therefore did not give full consideration to what is involved in Christian love. Even so, his argument demands the closest attention. To answer it in full would take us far beyond the scope of this book. It would require a much completer knowledge of psychoanalysis than we can presume. But we can at least indicate the lines along which the answer is to be found.

In the first place, Freud put forward the criticism tentatively. It was a conclusion towards which available evidence seemed to him to be pointing, and not one that he could overwhelmingly demonstrate from clinical evidence. We have already seen that he had a limited knowledge of the essential features of true Christianity and a deeper acquaintance with it might have led him to change his mind. He regarded Christianity as a system of beliefs and conduct to be imposed upon the individual, rather than as an inner growth of the self, a transformation of the personality. Secondly, psychoanalysis is not the only science of which Christianity must take account as a source of factual knowledge. It must, for instance, give heed to the lessons of history. It was from their reflection over history that the great Hebrew prophets gained their insights which prepared the way for Christianity. If these other sciences lead to the Christian faith that man can only attain his highest development when he is moved entirely by love, then Christians are quite justified in asking psychoanalysts to re-examine their evidence. Thirdly, and this seems to be particularly pertinent to the conclusions we have drawn in this book, Freud can be pitted against Freud. The general body of psychoanalytic findings about the growth of the human mind indicates a norm of human development whose characteristic is the harmonious functioning of Id, Ego, and Super-ego under the leadership of the Ego. As we have seen, it is just such a character that Jesus appears to have displayed and to have sought to foster in his followers. What aggressiveness was manifested by him was not in opposition to, but subordinate to, an overriding purpose of love, and in the very situations where, according to Freud, we might have anticipated aggressive reactions on his part, they are totally absent. If, therefore, Jesus does represent the psychological norm of development, represented by the freedom of his Ego, it would suggest that Freud, in pursuing the particular problem of the handling of aggression, has not fully grasped the implications of his main work.

There is, therefore, plenty of reason to doubt the validity of Freud's argument that Christianity is asking the impossible. It still remains to see in what way Freud was wrong. The methods of handling aggression have to be discovered and this will be a major task of psychologists in the future. Much attention is being given to it by some of Freud's followers. The outcome of their further investigations is certain to require considerable modifications in Christian thought and practice. Already it is clear that Christianity cannot be content with a simple denial of aggression and with preaching a milk and water attitude to life. Christianity must be full-blooded, and not merely must it find expression in its love for the passionate devotion of the sex instincts, and their creative upsurge, it must also take on the quality of fierceness that belongs to the aggressive instincts.

If psychoanalysis helps to clear away the rubbish that clings to Christianity and frees it to grow to its full strength and maturity, it will do it an immeasurable service. If Christianity insists on clinging to neurotic manifestations of the un-conscious as true religion for full-grown men and women it dooms itself to be cast aside in man's upward struggle towards the natural goals of freedom, power and love. It will cease to be truly 'Christian'.

FOR FURTHER READING

Of works by Sigmund Freud the beginner will probably find the following most useful, especially if read in this order:

The Psychopathology of Everyday Life (Fisher Unwin, 1914)
Introductory Lectures on Psychoanalysis (Allen and Unwin, 1922)
An Autobiographical Study (Hogarth Press, 1935)
Totem and Taboo (Routledge, 1919)
A General Selection from the Works of Sigmund Freud. Ed. John
    Rickman (Hogarth Press, 1937). This contains a number of
    important essays by Freud and the following, which have
    also been published as separate books:
  Beyond the Pleasure Principle (Hogarth Press, 1922)
  Group Psychology and the Analysis of the Ego (Hogarth Press,
    1922)
  The Ego and the Id (Hogarth Press, 1927)
  Inhibitions, Symptoms and Anxiety (Hogarth Press, 1937)
    It also contains an almost complete list of English trans-
    lations of Freud's writings.
The Future of an Illusion (Hogarth Press, 1928)
Civilisation and Its Discontents (Hogarth Press, 1930)
New Introductory Lectures on Psychoanalysis (Hogarth Press,
    1933)

For full study, the following should also be read:

The Interpretation of Dreams (Allen and Unwin, 1913)
Collected Papers (Hogarth Press, Vols. I and II, 1924; Vols. III
    and IV, 1925; Vol. V, 1950)
Various essays published elsewhere, to which reference may be
    found in the *General Selection* from Freud's works (see above)
Moses and Monotheism (Hogarth Press, 1939)
Psychoanalysis and Faith: Letters of S. Freud and O. Pfister
    (Hogarth Press, 1965)
Ernest Jones, *Sigmund Freud: Life and Work*, 3 vols. (Hogarth
    Press, 1953-7). (Edited and abridged by Lionel Trilling and
    Steven Marcus in 1 vol., *Life and Work of Sigmund Freud*,
    Pelican, 1964)

On Christianity the range of literature is too vast to make a general selection, but the following short statements are specially recommended:

T. R. Glover, *The Jesus of History* (S.C.M., 1917)
C. H. Dodd, *The Gospel and the Law of Christ. William Ainslie Memorial Lecture, 1946* (Longmans, Green & Co., 1947)

On the relations between psychology and religion:

L. W. Grensted, *Psychology and God. Bampton Lectures for 1930* (Longmans, Green & Co., 1930); *The Psychology of Religion* (H.U.L., O.U.P., 1952)
R. S. Lee, *Psychology of Worship* (S.C.M., 1953); *Your Growing Child and Religion* (Pelican, 1965)
Gregory Zilboorg, *Psychoanalysis and Religion* (Farrar, Strauss & Cudahy, 1962)

For developments in psychoanalytic thinking:

J. A. C. Brown, *Freud and the Post-Freudians* (Pelican, 1961)
Edith Jacobson, *The Self and the Object World* (Hogarth Press, 1965)
D. W. Winnicott, *The Family and Individual Development* (Hogarth Press, 1965); *The Maturational Processes and the Facilitating Environment* (Hogarth Press, 1965)

INDEX

179

MORE ABOUT PENGUINS
AND PELICANS

If you have enjoyed reading this book you may wish to know that *Penguin Book News* appears every month. It is an attractively illustrated magazine containing a complete list of books published by Penguins and still in print, together with details of the month's new books. A specimen copy will be sent free on request.

Penguin Book News is obtainable from most bookshops; but you may prefer to become a regular subscriber at 3s. for twelve issues. Just write to Dept EP, Penguin Books Ltd, Harmondsworth, Middlesex, enclosing a cheque or postal order, and you will be put on the mailing list.

Some other books published by Penguins are described on the following pages.

Note: *Penguin Book News* is not
available in the U.S.A., Canada or Australia.

THE SURVIVAL OF GOD IN THE SCIENTIFIC AGE

ALAN ISAACS

Is there a God?

On the one hand we have man's obstinate faith in the existence of God, a faith so powerful that, as Voltaire said, 'If God did not exist, it would be necessary to invent him.'

Against this stands the evidence of modern science – physics, biology, cosmology, explaining in its own terms the universe and the presence within it of life. With their observations on human thinking and behaviour, psychology and philosophy frequently confirm the findings of science.

In this volume Alan Isaacs reviews the opposing cases. For many he sees religious faith as a private necessity: for society as a whole, even in the nuclear age, he acknowledges that the concept of God may serve a useful function in the enforcement of moral codes. And if his conclusion is a frank 'I don't know', his path to it follows the profoundest issue of this, or any, age through the whole spectrum of twentieth-century thought.

WORLD RELIGIONS:
A DIALOGUE

NINIAN SMART

If religion is largely founded on faith, and faith on revelation, which of all the revelations are we to believe? Why make the Christian leap of faith, rather than the Muslim or Buddhist one?

Very different answers to such questions would be given in different parts of the world. And in this imaginative addition to the comparative study of religions Ninian Smart has adopted the form of a dialogue between a Christian, a Jew, a Muslim, a Hindu, and two Buddhists (from Ceylon and Japan) to demonstrate how the most influential creeds differ and on what they are agreed.

The result is a fresh and at times surprising insight into the religions of the world, as the protagonists exchange their fundamental beliefs about God and the Trinity, salvation, incarnation, good and evil.

FREUD AND THE
POST-FREUDIANS

J. A. C. BROWN

Freud and the Post-Freudians explains the main concepts
of Freudian psychology and goes on to review the
theories of Adler, Jung, Rank, and Stekel. Later
developments in the orthodox Freudian school are also
discussed, as are those of the American Neo-Freudians
and Post-Freudians in England.

This is the first book published in Britain to bring
together all these psychological and sociological schools
and criticize them, both from the Freudian standpoint
and that of the scientific psychologists.

THE LIFE AND WORK OF
SIGMUND FREUD

ERNEST JONES

'Truly monumental . . . a book that unquestionably ranks as one of the great biographies of our time . . . a classic such as this exceeds all just expectations.'

Such was the *New Statesman*'s final assessment of Ernest Jones's three-volume life of Freud. Of this abridgement, with its new introduction by Lionel Trilling, the same journal wrote: 'The editors have performed the operation well, with the care and respect due to a work of such permanent importance.'

We now have, in a single volume, the full story of Freud's personal struggle as well as his public successes – a story which reveals the extraordinary power and purpose with which he developed his scientific and artistic genius. It is an account which must be of the first interest not only to the student and professional psychologist but also to anyone who wishes properly to understand one of the most critical reorientations of thought in the history of civilization.

Not for sale in the U.S.A.